Words That Proceed

97 "Right Now" Devotions for Your Life Today

WES RALEY

ISBN: 1096898330

ISBN-13: 9781096898337

10 9 8 7 6 5 4 3 2 1

Dedication

This book is dedicated to my two sons, Isaac and Luke. May you one day become men in pursuit of the Living Word. May you delight in the thing that God is *currently* saying, be open to His counsel, and follow His direction. As your father, it's a paradigm I treasure deeply—the sons seeking the face and voice of their father. You have my love and my highest hopes that you will go far beyond me in everything God has graciously allowed me to do so far in my life, and may you be true men of God, not content to settle for clinging to "more of the same" but recognizing your deep need for the fresh daily manna from God, just as Jesus Himself said, "Man shall not live by bread alone, but by every **word that proceeds** from the mouth of God" (Matthew 4:4 NKJV). May you two become men who hunger for and are filled with the Bread of Life.

"So He humbled you, allowed you to hunger, and fed you with manna which you did not know nor did your fathers know, that He might make you know that man shall not live by bread alone; but man lives by every word that proceeds from the mouth of the LORD." **Deuteronomy 8:3 NKJV**

Table Of Contents

Acknowledgements

I want to specifically thank speaker and author Kris Vallotton for his introduction to the concept of "words that proceed" from God rather than simply "words that precede" or clinging to things of the past in place of a fresh daily word from the Living Word. Thank you Kris!

Foreword

He's an "on-time" God, yes He is.

I remember the first time I experienced this fact for myself. There I was, a former minister, condemned to prison, with an unspeakable amount of damage in my wake. Having lost my family, career, and I feared even my relationship with Jesus, I wondered if God's words had fallen flat. My shame had me believing that His calling on my life had gone down with His empty words.

"To the Lamb who was slaughtered before the world was made" Revelation 13:8 (NLT).

That means that before there was *time* or a *direction* to be known, the Word of God was sent out to accomplish the great mystery of bridging the gap between God and man. This gap in my own life, I believed, was too big to cross.

Before the division had even been made, a Word was set on an unstoppable course into eternity. By the grace of God, the Proceeding, Active, Alive Word intersected with my life.

"In the beginning was the Word...He was with God in the beginning" (John 1:1-2).

The Word personified is the Man Jesus Christ.

So there I was—a former minister—in prison. All morning long I lay in my bunk hearing a song play in my head, "You will seek but you'll never find God. Craig, it's over. You're done. Try as hard as you may—you won't find God." I couldn't take it anymore. "God!" I cried, "You hear this. I can't take this anymore. If there is anything you want me to know, I could really use it now or else I am just going to give up."

With my pink and brown leather Bible in my hands, I flopped it open on my lap. The very first words I read jumped off the page and choked the lies in my mind—crashing into my soul like a tidal wave in the desert.

"'You will seek me and find me when you seek me with all of your heart. I will be found by you,' declares the LORD, 'and I will bring you back from your captivity'" (Jeremiah 29:13-14).

A timely moment from a Word, spoken millennia before, to meet me at *that moment*...and it continues on. After that encounter, I have never been the same. I began to see that my Father in Heaven truly loves and cares for me.

Do you need that Word today? Do you need a fresh word from the God who is deeply in love with your heart and soul? If so, you've come to the right starting point.

My friend, Wes Raley, has played a major role in my reconnecting to God in desperate seasons by pointing me to the Words That Proceed—those spoken by Yahweh and lived out in the man Jesus Christ—currently representing, reminding and restoring by the Holy Spirit.

Here are some of the most simple and profound moments for your days. May you seek God, may you find Him, and may you hear His Words That Proceed. Maybe the next time you pick this book up you will have an encounter with God like I did. Let Him in, hear His Words and believe.

He's an "on-time" God, yes He is!

Craig Burden
May 2019

Author's Note

While you hope this would be true of every book you have the privilege to write, I have to say, this felt like a very special project that I believe God led me to. It was one of the most joy-filled and enjoyable books I've had the chance to work on. And while each book has a special place in your heart, there's something about *Words That Proceed* that will always be precious to me. I think that is due, in part, to how it came about. I never tried to crank out 97 devotions. I simply started writing down the things that I felt God was showing me or laying on my heart on a daily basis. I did this until I felt like God was leading me to a new season of rest and refreshment—a time to not have any "irons in the fire" so to speak. At any rate, I didn't know what to do with these very meaningful devotional thoughts until my wife and I took time to get away together and seek God's next steps for our lives. That's when we got a clear confirmation to *go forward* with this devotional out of a Kingdom principle: "Go with what you *do* have." One aspect that the Parable of the Talents shows us (Matthew 25:14-30) is that sometimes we can become overwhelmed by how many things *could* be done or by what we think we *lack* that we fail to invest what *has* been placed in our own hands (Exodus 4:2). So instead of trying to make *Words That Proceed* a 365 day devotional or something more complete, like 100 days, I simply went with what I had—97 "right now" devotions. I present this to you as a project of contentment and trust in the LORD—not waiting until something is *perfect* in our minds before *advancing* what we *do* have. May this devotional lead you to the same conclusion, that God isn't asking us to focus on what we *don't* have, but on what we *do*—and with eyes fixed on Jesus, we will share in His joy (Hebrews 12:2).

God bless you,
Wes Raley

Words That Proceed

97 "Right Now" Devotions for Your Life Today

Introduction: What Is God <u>Currently</u> Saying?

There are times in all of our lives where we are awakened to the reality of our true condition apart from God. It is in these moments that we recognize our helplessness and need for Him to move on our behalf. In these moments, the veil is lifted, and we see our true *need* for God.

Thankfully, God is faithful, and He saves everyone who calls upon His name (Acts 2:21). But it's critical to understand that what's gained in these desperate moments isn't simply deliverance from a problem but instruction about how we are to live a life of faith—with *complete dependence* upon Him. We should approach our days as if we actually do *need* Him...*because we actually do need Him.* In fact, we don't just need Him to *act* on our behalf, we need Him to *speak.* Jesus tells us that it is by His *current spoken word* (rhema) that we are fed: "But He answered and said, 'It is written, "MAN SHALL NOT LIVE ON BREAD ALONE, BUT ON EVERY WORD THAT PROCEEDS OUT OF THE MOUTH OF GOD"'" (Matthew 4:4 NASB).

It's not enough to live by words that "precede" or things that have gone by. We must have daily fresh words that "proceed" or emit right from the heart and mouth of God—we all need fresh manna daily (Deuteronomy 8:3).

Faith itself has one critical component: "Faith comes from hearing, and hearing through the word of Christ" (Romans 10:17 ESV). So hear's the question: How can we expect to be a people of *faith* if we are not listening, expecting, and hungering for God to speak?

This is the heart behind *Words That Proceed.*

My firm belief is that God still speaks today, as evidenced all throughout Scripture, but most assuredly when Jesus tells us, "My sheep hear my voice" (John 10:27 ESV). Even Paul told us that the reality we currently live in on earth is one where God desires that we might "reach toward Him" (Acts 17:27). I love how the ESV puts that same verse, "that they should seek God, and perhaps feel their way toward Him and find Him. Yet He is actually not far from each one of us" (Acts 17:27 ESV).

Powerful stuff! *God is not far from each one of us, and His desire is that we would feel our way toward Him.*

The idea of having a current relationship with God should not be doctrinally shaking to anyone—for the real danger would be knowing *about the Bible* but not knowing *God Himself as a Person* (Matthew 7:21-23). This, then, would be to partake of the error of the Pharisees who "studied the Scriptures diligently" but missed Jesus (John 5:39-40).

My hope is that these 97 devotions will be a tool for you to experience the intimacy that comes with drawing near to God and Him drawing near in return (James 4:8). May you not settle for what your yesterday's held or what God has done in the past, but may you, with the wisdom Jesus offers us, *reach toward Him* and seek "every word that proceeds out of the mouth of God" (Matthew 4:4 NASB).

May this devotional give you powerful insight about what to do when you don't know what to do and connect you to the heart, mind, and voice of the Living Word who speaks to us—not just in the past—but *right now*, today, and forever (Hebrews 13:8).

"Remember not the former things, nor consider the things of old. Behold, I am doing a new thing; now it springs forth, do you not perceive it? I will make a way in the wilderness and rivers in the desert" (Isaiah 43:18-19 ESV).

01
God's Question

"Do you do well to be angry?" ***Jonah 4:9 ESV***

It's really a simple question. But the profound part of it is that God is the one asking the question. It's a question you would think we would ask very little ones as they try to figure out what works and what doesn't work, what helps and what hinders in their choices and attitudes.

The question is basically this: Does it help you to get angry? Has it ever increased the pleasure, the joy, the blessings, the outcome? Does it do you any good personally to get angry?

So simple. Yet so profound.

The question comes to Jonah, a prophet, who didn't want the assignment he was given. And, after seeing mercy triumph over judgment in the lives of the people he wanted God to punish, Jonah pulled up a chair hoping that God would still enact judgment on the people around him.

Pulling up chairs and waiting for God to judge can be a wearisome task—especially with a heart set on finding pleasure in the downfall of others.

In the midst of this moment, God grows up a plant to shield Jonah.

All of God's instructions to us about anger are just as simple.

"Do not let the sun go down while you are still angry, and do not give the devil a foothold" (Ephesians 4:26-27).

Translation: Don't let this season, day, moment pass in anger. Don't let anger settle in your heart. Don't let the night seasons foster a heart of bitterness. Or, Satan will get in. He will get in your affairs, your relationships, your finances, your livelihood.

In other words—it doesn't do you well to get angry.

Please note, the brother of Jesus puts it this way, "Human anger does not produce the righteousness that God desires" (James 1:20).

If you want God's outcome for the situation, if you want His desire, if you want His will to come to pass—partnering with an angry, bitter spirit is not the answer.

No, God, to answer Your question, we don't do well to be angry.

02
Human Capacity

> *"Unless the LORD builds the house, those who build it labor in vain."* ***Psalm 127:1 ESV***

The mere fact that a house needs built is never an indicator that *you* are supposed to build it. No, a need does not always constitute a call. We are not supposed to live and work as if the building depends on us—as if we are the "saviors."

But oh the difference of when the LORD actually does build the house and our labor is not in vain! This "keeping in step with the Spirit" (Galatians 5:25 ESV) may be less mystical than I think then. It may have more to do with the *humility* of recognizing my *capacity*. Yes, there are limits to our humanity that are not to be aimlessly denied.

And while "I can do all things through Christ who strengthens me" (Philippians 4:13 ESV), I am very clearly not called to do *all* things. It has been well said before, "whatever He calls me to, He will equip me for." True. But can't it be said that the side of the fence we fall on is living like He has equipped us for *all* things instead of *called* things?

May God give us the grace to know our capacity, to not live like it all depends on us, and to step forward in great faith when we have the clarity of a calling but feel lacking in our abilities.

May our focus never be on lack, but always on our Great God and King, who is able to do more than we could ask, think, or imagine (Ephesians 3:20). But may we not *imagine* more than He has actually called us to. May we be good stewards of what He has given us, and not try to walk with both hands full (Ecclesiastes 4:6).

To Him be the glory!

03
Be Still

"Be still and know that I am God." **Psalm 46:10**

It is *imperative*. As in "you must." And the first imperative enables the second.

The first? Be *still* and then, you'll *know*. You cannot complete the second step of a scavenger hunt before the first.

Put quite simply: There is a knowledge of God that can only be found in stillness—and not just *in* stillness but stillness *in you*.

"Be still" is talking about your state of *being*.

"Still yourself" could be another way of saying it. So the imperative is firstly intentional—a choice.

The man after God's own heart knew this well: "I have calmed and quieted my soul" (Psalm 131:2 ESV). Notice *who* did it. Just like the contrast between Martha and Mary (Luke 10:38-42), knowing God in a deeper way comes with a *choice* —be still...

04
Different Seasons

"For His anger lasts only a moment, but His favor lasts a lifetime." ***Psalm 30:5***

It's very hard to calculate seasons.

Both naturally and spiritually—some seasons feel short while others feel like they will never end. Figuring out when your next breakthrough is coming or how much longer a difficult season will last can be an arduous and fruitless task.

Possibly because Jesus told us that it is not our task to undertake. "It is not for you to know the times or seasons that the Father has fixed by His own authority" (Acts 1:7 ESV).

But the *season* of walking in God's *favor*?

That lasts for a lifetime.

05
Triumph!

"But thanks be to God, who in Christ always leads us in triumphal procession." **2 Corinthians 2:14 ESV**

It's surprising.

He always leads us in triumph. A procession marching forward.

Why is it surprising?

Well, sometimes the world likes to paint God with a brush that makes Him seem comfortable with loss, okay with defeat, and apathetic toward victory. Even further, sometimes Christians paint God with a brush that He is not only comfortable with loss but *happy* with it. As if the losses and disappointments should be celebrated. Disappointment has been heralded in Christian circles almost as if it is a virtue.

But God leads us in *triumph*! What of the defeats of the past, you ask? Good question, what of them? For God is leading us ever upward, always toward the door He has placed before us that no one can shut (Revelation 3:8).

He is working all things for our good (Romans 8:28), and He is not preparing us for a life or a destiny of disappointment and defeat but one word: TRIUMPH.

He always leads us in triumph. May we view Him in that light, and may we keep in step with Him, going in the direction called "forward" (Exodus 14:15 ESV). May the victory He brings into your life surprise you as well, not because you thought it out of line with His character, but because the kind of victory He brings is so constant and so generous that it may surprise you in the amount and frequency of triumph into which He leads you. Joyful laughter is an appropriate response. May you have days ahead of jumping for joy at the fruition of your faith in a God who has promised us victory and rest on every side (Joshua 21:44)!

06
Aversion to Boredom

> *"In quietness and trust shall be your strength."*
> ***Isaiah 30:15 ESV***

Boredom, then, doesn't appear to be so much of a problem but perhaps, rather, a solution. And, the bypass of busyness and overt aversion to boredom may actually be a perpetuation of the problem. For if we find God in stillness (Psalm 46:10), how could we ever seek to know Him deeper by distracting ourselves from what we fear to be a terrible state—*boredom*—with nothing else to do?

Not that stillness is boredom—not at all. Rather, the mindset that Satan wants us to develop is one of "progress at all costs" and "activity without stillness." Boredom is a word from his vocabulary uttered to make us fear ourselves into activity.

I've talked to many people about something so simple as even taking one day off each week (not an original idea by the way), and their responses have been very telling: "But what would we *do* all day?"

My response? "Exactly!"

May God give us the wisdom to understand what past generations seemed to know instinctively—that boredom is not our enemy and that having nothing to do can actually lead to our greatest accomplishments.

07

Where Are You Leaning?

> *"Trust in the LORD with all your heart, and do not lean on your own understanding..."* ***Proverbs 3:5 ESV***

Faith, as it is defined for us in scripture— the conviction of things not seen (Hebrews 11:1)—is not only measured by what we *do* (ie taking a "step" of faith) but also by what we *don't* do.

Often we think of faith in terms of *acts* of faith. Something that took tremendous trust in God to carry out.

But sometimes trust in the LORD is often compelled to *not* do things.

For example, "Do not lean..." (Proverbs 3:5 ESV).

In this case, do not lean on your own *understanding*.

What does this suggest? It suggests going against the natural course of action. It suggests "not doing" something when you are trained to do the very thing you are being asked not to do. What's that thing? Leaning on, relying on, operating by what you seem to understand.

Is the instruction given because our understanding is flawed? Not necessarily. It does not mean we have to *distrust* our understanding, it means we must not *lean* on it. Instead, we are to place our trust in another Source, God Himself.

Consider the faith it takes to NOT do some things: To not respond fear, to not respond in anger, to not respond in a controlling way, to not respond at all...

Many times when our circumstances do not line up with our ideals, we resort to fear, anger, control, and manipulation to try to make things go back in line with what we desire. That's what our understanding tells us to do. But faith of the Biblical nature and which God desires for us, chooses—almost foolishly so—to *not do* some things. What is it that you have been doing out of a spirit of fear, anger, control, or manipulation?

May we be the kind of people whose trust in God far exceeds the weight we place upon what we think we understand. May we be the kind of people who choose the "not doing" of faith, as God leads.

08
Mercy Triumphs

> *"For judgment is without mercy to one who has shown no mercy."* ***James 2:13 ESV***

It's a sobering thought. But even more sobering when I realize that this is not just a *thought* but a *principle.*

The way principles work are kind of scary. They operate in the background whether you know they exist or not. In other words, you could be completely oblivious to a principle but still reap the consequences in your life.

This principle? The measure of mercy you give others is the one you're going to receive.

Judgment from whom? That's a good question. And I don't know entirely, which makes this principle all the more sobering. The point really isn't *where* we will receive the judgment but simply *that* we will.

In the moment, when I am tempted toward judgment—when I harshly come down on someone's actions, heart, motives, character...I could actually be 100% right yet with the wrong heart.

Really the whole question is: Is the harshness with which I am coming down on that person the *exact* same way I am desiring to be treated? Because you will be given the exact same measure in due course.

How do I know that?

"So in everything, do to others what you would have them do to you" (Matthew 7:12).

Why? Because that's what will happen—it will be done unto you. The same measure is given over to you, whether you act with judgment or with mercy.

The good news is that principles are always twofold—the consequences and the benefits. How can you use this principle to your advantage? Recognize that if you want your life to operate *under* mercy you've got to operate *from* mercy.

How do I know that? Because James the brother of Jesus goes on in the same verse quoted above to say, "Mercy triumphs over judgment" (James 2:13 ESV). That's the only way you win.

So are you fixated on a person, problem, action, or hurt? Or, are you fixated on mercy? There's no middle ground. Well, I guess there are degrees. You could call them "measures." Jesus said it that way in the book of Matthew, "For with the judgment you pronounce you will be judged, and with the *measure* you use it will be *measured* to you" (Matthew 7:2 ESV).

Only mercy will triumph over judgment, both in the lives of the people around you and in your own, for we find from these verses that the two are inextricably linked.

09
Grace Upon Grace

> *"For from His fullness we have all received, grace upon grace."* ***John 1:16 ESV***

Who has received? We *all* have.

What's the implication? We *all* need.

We all need grace. And not just grace, but grace *upon* grace. Often, when I have *given* grace, I think the next thing I must give is something entirely different. If someone needs grace from me, and they do it again, my assumption is not to stack grace *upon* grace.

And not just people but situations. Sometimes things can become so tangled—we must remember that there is no rule book we operate by. "For all who are led by the Spirit of God are sons of God" (Romans 8:14 ESV). We are led by the Spirit, not logic or natural course. And it's a good thing. Because being led by anything or anyone else would not produce fruit such as love, joy, peace, patience, kindness, goodness, faithfulness, gentleness, and self-control (Galatians 5:22-23).

But if we are to be led by the Spirit, the same way Jesus was, then we are to transmit the same: grace *upon* grace. The tricky part is not giving grace, the tricky part is when it's grace *upon* grace. May we be a people who are wise enough to realize that the only way to live a life of grace is explicitly as John told us "from His fullness" (John 1:16). Be filled today by not just His grace, but grace *upon* grace.

10

God's Method of Motivation

> *"There is no fear in love, but perfect love casts out fear. For fear has to do with punishment, and whoever fears has not been perfected in love."*
> ***1 John 4:18 ESV***

Fear has to do with punishment.

Yes, God's love casts out all fear.

Is there any measure of my perceived relationship with God that is based on the fear of punishment?

Do I interact with, serve, love, give, or sacrifice because I am *afraid* of what will happen if I don't?

Although the above verses have so many beautiful avenues of practicality, they couldn't be clearer: *God does not motivate us with fear.*

The places in our lives that are motivated by the fear of punishment are under the influence of the demonic.

God's love casts fear out, *if* you'll receive His love. But nothing will change until we change our minds (Romans 12:2) about God and His heart toward us.

Why the fear? God's Word makes clear that:

"God is love" (1 John 4:8 ESV).

"God's *kindness* is meant to lead you to repentance" (Romans 2:4 ESV). Note: It does NOT read: "His *punishment* leads us to repentance."

Finally, may this prayer echo in your heart today: "I pray that out of His glorious riches He may strengthen you with power through His Spirit in your inner being, so that Christ may dwell in your hearts through faith. And I pray that you, being *rooted and established in love*, may have power, together with all the Lord's holy people, *to grasp how wide and long and high and deep is the love of Christ*, and *to know this love* that surpasses knowledge—*that you may be filled* to the measure of all the fullness of God" (Ephesians 3:16-19).

His love changes *everything*.

11
It's Your Choice

> *"Let patience have her perfect work."* ***James 1:4 KJV***

James the brother of Jesus makes us acutely aware of the purpose of pain. He speaks of trials as things to be celebrated (James 1:2)—not because of their nature or origin but because of the sure fruit that will come *if...*

If what?

If we *let* patience have her perfect work (James 1:4 KJV).

The implication is that we have a *choice*. We can try to rush through this season, quickly conquer the problem, or take the easy way out. Or, we can *let* patience have her way.

Patience and slowness just seem to go hand in hand. It's not that trying to overcome a difficulty is a problem—no for Jesus came to bear our burdens and set the captives free (Isaiah 61:1). The problem is that we often want to wriggle out from underneath pressure. We want to speed through to the fruit before we have any semblance of endurance.

It's probably why the writer of Hebrews said: "You have need of endurance, so that when you have done the will of God you may receive what is promised" (Hebrews 10:36 ESV).

But patience has a perfect work to complete.

I find it interesting that the King James Version ascribes "patience" a feminine gender. "Let patience have *her* perfect work" (James 1:4 KJV). To me, this opens the door to character qualities not normally ascribed to a man. Things like beauty, elegance, and tenderness are represented in that word which otherwise may not be.

Yes, patience and slowness seem to go hand in hand. Can we see the beauty, elegance, and tenderness of the patience at work in the pain?

If so, may we be the kind of people who don't run from pressure but allow slowness to trump quick results in our fast-paced, instant-rewards society. May we trust that there is a beauty, elegance, and tenderness at work, even when we cannot see it.

12
The Father's Heart

"He does not reward us according to our iniquities."
Psalm 103:10 AMPC

God does not measure out blessings based on what we've done wrong.

This passage clearly shows that God is a loving Father. He has compassion on us as His children. He cares about how we feel. He cares about all we go through. And, when it comes to us seeing our destiny come to pass, not once has God rewarded us according to our wrongdoing.

Just as any good father would seek the success and ultimate fulfillment of their children, so too our God in Heaven is not looking to condemn or withhold from us.

This hits home in a big way when we feel weighed down for messing up. Do we view God as someone who is mad and aloof shouting something like, "Well, you lost it all! There goes your destiny! It's over for you!" Or, do we view Him in line with the revelation Jesus gave us of a Father who is not ashamed to *run* after His child, however wayward he once was, and reward him—no—*shower* him with rewards and blessings unimaginable (Luke 15:20)?

This image is inconceivable to the religious-minded person who, with the older brother of the story, would stay out of the party simply because someone else was not rewarded according to their *iniquities*.

Yet such is the heart of our Father.

13
Striving vs. Resting

"Better is a handful of quietness than two hands full of toil and a striving after wind." **Ecclesiastes 4:6 ESV**

The implied truth here is that nothing will stop you from doing the latter even if the former is eternally better. The only thing that may stop you are the consequences of living a life of striving and chasing after the wind. In such cases, perhaps the consequences could be viewed as God's grace, if such consequences result in the former, a handful of quietness. Not that the consequences should be welcomed, and certainly not that they should stay, but hasn't it been true in your life, Christian, that when you've found yourself weary and weak, burnt out and overwhelmed, that the Savior's offer of rest has become precious to you? Hasn't there met once in your life a wall of resistance which has shown you that the way of the world truly is death?

There is so much you could chase after. And, according to this verse the image of one handful of quietness would leave one hand open to receive the work and progress the LORD desires. But when we try to get it all...when we try to *find* our lives, as Jesus said, we *lose* them (Matthew 10:39). A simple, quiet contentment without trying to get our fill of all that we could ever have in terms of "success" or "progress" will lead to a life of true joy and satisfaction in our Lord Jesus.

So much could be done. So much could be pursued. And, other than the consequences of your own limited capacity, you could go for it all. But truly, are you someone who desires to be led by consequences or led by the Holy Spirit?

Wisdom from God gives us the *grace* to know when we should "be still and know that He is God" (Psalm 46:10), long before the consequences *force* us to.

14
God's Will

> *"The mind of man plans his way, But the LORD directs his steps."* ***Proverbs 16:9 NASB***

We should not, therefore, be disappointed when our plans do not go "according to plan." There is a divine plan which is higher and altogether better for us.

And, though we cannot fully fathom the ways of a God whose thoughts are higher than our thoughts (Isaiah 55:9), we can trust, however naive the world may rate us, that God will in fact work all things together for our good (Romans 8:28).

This then is our hope, that when our plans fail, our hope was not in our *plans* but in the *God* who orders our steps according to His divine will, which thankfully will always work for our good.

Letting go to this reality is one of the most freeing experiences in life. It is a prerequisite to maturing in our walk with the LORD. We are not in control, and though God gives us great liberty to plan our way, ultimately it is He who directs our steps.

May we perceive the gentleness and lovingkindness of God today knowing that our steps are ordered according to His plan and not our own.

15
Discernment to Desist

> *"Do not toil to acquire wealth; be discerning enough to desist."* ***Proverbs 23:4 ESV***

We all have a capacity.

We also all have a choice.

Will we live as if we have to have the *full amount* that we can? Or will we show discernment and be wise enough to desist knowing that "each day has enough" (Matthew 6:34)?

The implication of this verse is that there is a magnetic pull trying to get you to *strive and toil* to accumulate what God actually wants to give you *effortlessly*.

"The blessing of the LORD makes rich, and toil adds nothing to it" (Proverbs 10:22 ESV).

When we shift into the flesh, we think that we have to keep striving to make sure we get the most that we can. But the Kingdom of God is often paradoxical, and that means that those who enter into true rest get both. They no longer have to strive and yet the blessing of the LORD makes rich.

This obviously isn't a call for us to live with apathy or laziness, but it is a call for us to live with abandon—to know our limits and be wise enough to desist, confident that all true blessings come from the LORD. He will add great things to the one who seeks Him first (Matthew 6:33)!

16
Do What You Wish They Had

"So in everything, do to others what you would have them do to you." ***Matthew 7:12***

Sometimes we see ourselves in others.

We know how they feel, for we ourselves have been in their situation before. In fact, we often avoid people who remind us of ourselves, whether in personality or circumstance.

Circumstantially, it's almost as if we don't want to go through something again that we've gone through before. Or we see their personality and can detect where they are lacking or hurting or failing or not understanding...and we distance ourselves.

But what if we purposed to do exactly what Jesus said? What if we did *to* or *for* this person what we wish someone would have done for us?

What if, the places where we felt abandoned or discouraged or dissociated from in the *past* became the very places we fill in the *present*—meeting the needs of the person before us that we wish would have been met by someone else for us? Doing to others *as* we'd have them do to us.

Let's go out of our way to do for that person what we wish we would have had done for us. This is, after all, what has been coined "The Golden Rule."

It is both redemptive and prophetic. Both what we wish others had done and how we'd like others to do. Then, to do it is an act of great faith.

For if we were to wait for others to do for us before we'd do for them, what kind of faith does that take? This is how the world operates every day.

May we find extreme joy (2 Corinthians 8:2) giving in an altogether different fashion than the world does—doing unto others *as* we'd have them do to us.

17
Jesus Said No

"He can do only what He sees His Father doing..."
John 5:19

The implication is that there are many things Jesus did *not* do.

So much needed to be done, it seemed. If there were anyone who felt the pressure of doing it all, it had to be Jesus. He was the one most capable of it, at the least. And, His love and compassion for the state of humanity topped anyone.

But He, even He made a choice. He only did what He saw His Father doing.

How strange then that Jesus, humanity's most significant Yes and Amen (2 Corinthians 1:20), by virtue of this choice, had to say *no*.

And it begs the question: If Jesus, even Jesus, had to say no to things, what makes us think that we will not? What makes us think we can do it all? And perhaps it's not even framed up in our mind that way, but isn't there a magnetic pull that makes you think it's all on you? That if you don't do it, no one will—or at the bare minimum—it won't get done the right way?

I think we all know that feeling. And, this verse begs the question, how should we know what we *are* to do?

If we seek to follow Jesus as our guide, the answer would be that we choose to do only the things we see our Father doing.

But that seems so spiritual that it's hard to put your finger on.

How do we practically *watch* what the Father is doing? Jesus' statement to Philip surely has some significance here: "Don't you know me, Philip, even after I have been among you such a long time? Anyone who has seen me has seen the Father" (John 14:9).

This is not meant to be a commentary on the Trinity in any fashion, but simply to see our need for Jesus to direct our days. As the writer of Hebrews puts it, "fixing our eyes on Jesus, the author and perfecter of faith..." (Hebrews 12:2 NASB).

What is Jesus' agenda for your day? I'm not so sure we always know ahead of time, but like Martha, I'm fairly certain we know afterward (Luke 10:42).

For chasing after those things in my flesh is seeking to be like those dispersed at Babel and moving on the motivation, "Let us make a name for ourselves" (Genesis 11:4 ESV). I know the emptiness which pursuing my own agenda brings. I know afterwards. I'm learning to know before.

May God give us spiritual eyes to know in advance the agenda He has for us, instead of spinning our wheels trying to follow something that might cross off a checklist but leave us feeling empty inside.

It would appear that like Martha, there is great value to us sitting at the feet of Jesus instead of busying ourselves with everything we *think* we are supposed to be doing (Luke 10:42).

18
Enough Is Enough!

"Each day has enough..." ***Matthew 6:34***

But many try to assign us more than that.

Even our own ideals of how our day should go often cross the threshold of "enough."

It's almost as if we think that if we don't *do* more than enough, we won't *be* enough.

And that's how we are trained.

We will never live with the peace that God intends for us to have if we refuse to be satisfied with days that are simply "enough."

May God give us the grace of living each day within the boundary and capacity He has set for our good. May we be satisfied with *enough*!

19
In Him

"And He is before all things, and in Him all things hold together." **Colossians 1:17 ESV**

Check the areas which are falling apart.

Where in your life do you need "holding together" today?

Family.
Finances.
Marriage.
Children.
Friendship.
Job.
Health.

Whatever area is specific to you, just make sure that it is "in Him."

The list is probably endless. What place in our lives wouldn't we desire Jesus to *hold together*? Truly, what kind of person actually wants things to fall apart?

This verse isn't a promise that things will always go perfectly. But it is a promise that all things hold together *in Jesus*. So, if it's not *in Jesus*, it's no wonder that it's not holding together.

I have met many men who were dating or married to someone and that relationship was falling apart. But they could not truly say that their marriage or relationship was defined as *in Him*.

The finances of many seem to be a never-ending rollercoaster. But the most important thing to ask is not what *investments* you plan on making but if your finances are *in Him*.

Sometimes that seems too ambiguous to grasp. What does it mean, exactly, to be *in Him*?

Don't miss the first part of this verse. "He is before all things" (Colossians 1:17 ESV).

The real question remains: *Is Jesus before all things to you*? Does He have first place not only in your heart but also in the places you are desiring Him to hold together?

When things are falling apart, it's the wisest thing to bring it to Jesus because *in Him*, all things hold together.

Let Him have first place and experience the security that His stability brings.

20
The Praise of Man

"For they loved human praise more than praise from God." ***John 12:43***

This one cuts deep.

It seems that we have a choice to make. What will we value more? Will we value human praise more than praise from God or God's praise more than praise from man?

If our focus is on the praise that comes from God and His favor in our lives, I believe that we will also find favor with man, just as Jesus grew in both (Luke 2:52).

But even in Jesus' case, His favor was first listed as with God. When we occupy ourselves and delight ourselves in His opinion of us, we may begin to find favor in unexpected places. But chasing down the praise of man often leaves us with emptiness in both! We are unaware of or unacquainted with God's true thoughts toward us, which leaves us feeling empty, and our best efforts at making another human praise us fall flat!

I believe that this is God's grace toward us. When we have wandered down the path of seeking the praise of man, He often allows us to hit bottom or experience the emptiness and insecurity that comes with such occupation. But that is only so that we can turn, embrace what is right, and experience the wholeness and security that comes from sole occupation with His praise, opinion, and thoughts toward us.

It's why a proper mindset listens for and looks forward to, "Well done, good and faithful servant!" (Matthew 25:23).

21
True Faith

> *"And without faith it is impossible to please God, because anyone who comes to Him must believe that He exists and that He rewards those who earnestly seek Him."* **Hebrews 11:6**

There is only one way to please God...faith.

And there are two conditions for faith:

1) *You must believe that God exists.*

Many meet this condition. Countless numbers of people believe that there *is* a God. Truth be told, if this were the only condition of faith, many people would meet this requirement, for even the demons do (James 2:19).

But that is not where faith stops. Faith is not simply about God's *existence* but His *character*. Notice the second condition of faith.

2) *You must believe that He rewards those who earnestly seek Him.*

God's nature is that of Rewarder.

Sadly, many in our culture and even in Christian circles have come to understand God as Punisher, but that is neither true nor a condition of faith.

It takes *no faith* to believe that bad things will happen. It takes *no faith* to believe that God will not come through. It takes *no faith* to believe that God exists but wants my suffering.

Faith believes that God both exists *and* wants my best.

This is why it is critical that we view God in light of Jesus' revelation to us—a Father who loves to give good gifts to His children (Matthew 7:11).

The enemy loves to twist thoughts about God and try to pervert our views of His nature. The enemy tries to get us to believe that God will not come through, doesn't care all that much, and is quick to reprimand us for wrong—even though the Word of God says that He is "slow to anger" (Exodus 34:6).

Has your view been that of faith or of doubt? Don't doubt God's goodness or His desires to come through for you! Don't let any sense of past disappointment temper your faith.

Are you anticipating good today or anticipating evil? This may give a picture of your view of God. You believe He exists, but in faith, will you also choose to believe that He is a Rewarder of those who seek Him?

May we seek Him today with the eyes of faith, joyfully anticipating good to happen because of God's nature and deeply intimate love as our Father.

22
God's Favor

"LORD, when You favored me, You made my royal mountain stand firm; but when You hid Your face, I was dismayed." ***Psalm 30:7***

The favor of the LORD can get us into places that we couldn't have gotten into ourselves and get us out of places that we have gotten ourselves into.

The presence of God's favor is life and light.

The absence of His favor is noticeable.

When God's favor is upon someone their "royal mountain stands firm" (Psalm 30:7). It's as if nothing at all can move them from their position. We call that being *established.*

But that same individual without God's favor is "dismayed" (Psalm 30:7). In our day we call that being *stressed.* It's because without God's favor we often resort to trying to produce on our own the same results that we would have had with His favor. That leads to a life of striving.

May we recognize that God's *favor* is what we need for every situation and relationship we encounter today and pray the same prayer that Moses did:

"Let the favor of the Lord our God be upon us, and establish the work of our hands upon us; yes, establish the work of our hands" (Psalm 90:17 ESV).

23
Stand on His Word

> *"With long life I will satisfy him and show him my salvation."* **Psalm 91:16 ESV**

When God gives a promise, Satan is most surely to try to oppose it. But the good news is, he is only able to oppose *appearances*. When he tries to make it seem like God will not come through—we have a choice.

Will we continue to believe what God has promised, or will we give way to fear?

Satan will threaten your life if you let him. He will whisper fearful words into your ears, but you have a choice to make!

Stand on God's promises and enjoy the fullness of what God has for you which includes living a life *free from fear*. If God promises you a long life, make sure you don't allow Satan to ruin it by making it a life filled with fear.

Things may appear threatening right now, but all that matters is what God has said. Don't let go of what He has said and you won't give way to fear.

Thank You, God, for your promises! Help me stand in faith when all seems lost and not cower to appearances that try to contradict your Word!

24
The Set Time

> *"But when the set time had fully come, God sent His Son, born of a woman, born under the law to redeem those under the law, that we might receive adoption to sonship."* ***Galatians 4:4-6***

The birth of Jesus has got to be one of the greatest proofs that the waiting *will* one day come to an end and God's promise *will* come to pass in our lives.

It is also proof that God Himself picks the number of days until fulfillment. While everything God does has purpose, sometimes the waiting is not due to anything we can figure out or change.

It is in theses moments that we are best to agree with Ezekiel and proclaim, "Oh LORD, you know" (Ezekiel 37:3) rather than live with the perpetual anxiety of trying to figure out what else you need to do to "make it happen" or "bring it to pass." For truly, only the LORD knows, and just as in the most important case in history—God sending His Son—sometimes it is simply about the fullness of *time* coming to pass.

This, then, is our great encouragement. God is not simply a Promiser. He is also a Father who sees His promise through to fulfillment. Just as at Christmastime we see, the waiting will come to an end, and in the fullness of time, "not one of all the LORD's good promises to Israel failed; every one was fulfilled" (Joshua 21:45).

And so it will be for us as well!

25
Higher Revelation

> *"Blessed are the pure in heart, for they will see God."*
> ***Matthew 5:8***

If you want a greater revelation of God, ask Him to purify your heart.

Is there nothing in your thought life, your desires, your activities or business transactions that could be more pure? Surely there is something, as you lay your life out openly before God, where you have not fully committed your heart to Him.

If you want the happiness that God has for you (for this is what the beatitudes teach us, the way of happiness or how to be "blessed"), then ask yourself the question, "How is my purity?"

God, today I simply seek Your face and ask You to expose all of the darkness in my heart with Your light. Fill me with Your love and revelation as I, one by one, surrender these areas afresh to You today, in Jesus' Name.

May we be "all in" for Him, not simply in our words or actions, but in the depths of our hearts. May our thoughts line up with His goodness, character, and truth. And may we be excited for purity and all of the joy that it brings!

26
Redeem the Time

"Redeeming the time, because the days are evil."
Ephesians 5:16 KJV

It might well be put, "Live in *this moment*, for the fleeting nature of things will try to pull you to miss your purpose."

The time we have today is the time we've been told to redeem, live in, be present in, enjoy, and be thankful for. Yet how often do the regrets of the past or the concerns for the future keep us from fully redeeming the moments we are in?

God, please give us the grace to live in the moment today and with the psalmist declare, "This is the day that the LORD has made; let us rejoice and be glad in it" (Psalm 118:24 ESV).

We are thankful for our yesterdays and hopeful about our tomorrows but not distracted from today. Help us, LORD, in all of our remembering and planning to not miss what is *right in front of us*, the gift of today! Amen!

27
Tenderhearted

> *"Be kind to one another, tenderhearted, forgiving one another, as God in Christ forgave you."* ***Ephesians 4:32 ESV***

I could say so many things about this wonderful verse. But all I want to point out is one little word, "tenderhearted."

It's really not a word we use in our normal conversations anymore. Just think about it, when was the last time you described someone as *tenderhearted*?

But even more convicting, when was the last time that you would have described that as *your* heart condition?

Tenderhearted.

It's a beautiful word.

As I look back on times where I regret what I said or how I acted, this one little word neither described my heart attitude nor my position before God. Most of the things I would take back in my life were due to not having this one thing.

Heart surgery in the natural is something that only the incredibly gifted can accomplish. And, in a real way, it's true of our soul. Only God can change a man's heart. But can we not choose to be in agreement with His handiwork? Can we not usher in His will by desire, proclamation, and agreement?

As we look back over the course of our lives, there will never be a time when we will have been sorry for being tenderhearted. To love as Christ loves is a miraculous thing, and we find that it is also God's will for us. He never wills something that He will not happily grant to those who come into agreement with Him.

It is possible for our hearts to break for the same things that His does.

We agree with You, Sovereign LORD. We want to be a people who are tenderhearted, loving and forgiving as You are. Help us to have the eyes to see that being tenderhearted is Your will, even when it's easier to rise up in anger or defensiveness. Soften our hearts today, LORD!

28
Letting Go

"For to set the mind on the flesh is death, but to set the mind on the Spirit is life and peace." ***Romans 8:6 ESV***

Sometimes we have to take our hands off of something before the LORD will place His hands on something.

There could be many reasons for this, but ultimately, I think it often boils down to trust. If we experience great success or breakthrough and think it was due to the toiling of our *own* hands, guess what we will try to reproduce?

When we operate with a mind set on the flesh, we will try to gain our purpose from toiling and striving. It literally is a *mindset*. But a mindset of the Spirit produces life and peace. Why? Because we are no longer striving but resting in His ability, care, leadership, guidance, and power.

It seems so simple: Would you rather have a life of effort and frustration or "life and peace" (Romans 8:6 ESV)? It boils down to this question: What is your mindset? Have you set your mind on all of your own efforts and plans? If so, please think rationally—why would God bring a breakthrough into your life which would only further solidify your lifestyle of self-reliance and distrust in Him?

It's a good question. It's a fair question. And, it's one that, if you'd give it room in your life, I'm confident God would use it to stir up your faith and bring you greater peace and joy in the Holy Spirit than you've had in any of the days where you sought to justify your existence or pursue your goals through self effort and determination.

God, help us choose to set our minds on the Spirit and not on the flesh. Give us holy mindsets today, in Jesus' Name. Amen!

29
Victory!

"But thanks be to God, who in Christ always leads us in triumphal procession..." **2 Corinthians 2:14 ESV**

God's nature is one of victory, not defeat.

And yet, if we're honest, we're inclined to live like the opposite is true—fearing the worst and envisioning loss.

But what happened to believing the best (1 Corinthians 13:7)? If it's a love *imperative* for us in our daily lives, shouldn't it be most true toward *God*?

The experiences and teachings of many have resulted in the disbelief of even clear scriptures like Psalm 91 which teaches:

"Whoever dwells in the shelter of the Most High will rest in the shadow of the Almighty" (Psalm 91:1).

"I will say of the LORD, 'He is my refuge and my fortress, my God, in whom I trust'" (Psalm 91:2).

"Surely He will save you from the fowler's snare and from the deadly pestilence" (Psalm 91:3).

"He will cover you with His feathers, and under His wings you will find refuge; His faithfulness will be your shield and rampart" (Psalm 91:4).

“You will not fear the terror of night, nor the arrow that flies by day, nor the pestilence that stalks in the darkness, nor the plague that destroys at midday” (Psalm 91:5-6).

“A thousand may fall at your side, ten thousand at your right hand, but it will not come near you. You will only observe with your eyes and see the punishment of the wicked” (Psalm 91:7-8).

“If you say, ‘The LORD is my refuge,’ and you make the Most High your dwelling, no harm will overtake you, no disaster will come near your tent” (Psalm 91:9-10).

“For He will command His angels concerning you to guard you in all your ways; they will lift you up in their hands, so that you will not strike your foot against a stone” (Psalm 91:11-12).

“You will tread on the lion and the cobra; you will trample the great lion and the serpent” (Psalm 91:13).

“‘Because he loves me,’ says the LORD, ‘I will rescue him; I will protect him, for he acknowledges my name’” (Psalm 91:14).

“‘He will call on me, and I will answer him; I will be with him in trouble, I will deliver him and honor him’” (Psalm 91:15).

“‘With long life I will satisfy him and show him my salvation’” (Psalm 91:16).

We are in great danger of error by allowing our experiences (or worse—the experiences of others) to shape our theology.

Word for today: *Victory*!

30
To Whom Shall We Go?

"And after the earthquake...a gentle whisper."
1 Kings 19:12

Has the loud and profound stolen your focus?

Has the pressure of performance and the shaking of urgency deafened your ability to hear?

It's an illustration of our modern times, but a good one—how many of us have been at a loud setting such as a concert and not been able to even hear the person next to us?

So then, proximity isn't necessarily the issue. You've got to learn to "be still" if you want to "know He is God" (Psalm 46:10).

There will always be sights and sounds which threaten to drown out His gentle quiet leading. But the discipline of training ourselves to listen and hear and distinguish His voice will prepare us to not be distracted by what appears urgent and consuming.

Sometimes we cannot hear God because of our relentless pursuits of "getting it all right"—just as Martha was distracted by such a great thing as serving (Luke 10:40).

God, give us the grace to quiet ourselves and hear Your voice today. We declare and agree with the disciples: "Lord, to whom shall we go? You have the words of eternal life" (John 6:68 ESV).

It is not always our *motives* which are off but perhaps our *methods* which are tied to our core beliefs. Namely, do we believe that God is waiting on us, or is *the real issue* that we have failed to wait on Him?

31
There's Always More

> *"Do not toil to acquire wealth; be discerning enough to desist." **Proverbs 23:4 ESV***

It's another way of saying, "there's always more that you *could* do." But how do you know when to stop? You need wisdom.

Clearly, our stopping is not explicitly tied to completion or perfection, for we see that God Himself didn't finish the work of creation on a single day but *chose a stopping point* every single day, and even a full day during that creation week (Genesis 1:1-31, 2:1-3).

So we are not to gauge our stopping on the perception of completion. We need the wisdom of the LORD to do what may seem foolish to the world and "quit while we're ahead." Or in a more real way, it may *feel* like "quitting while we're behind."

And while our purpose and our daily assignments will of course continue, we must be aware of the enemy's attempts to keep us constantly feeling like we are barely staying afloat, one unfinished task away from total failure.

The truth is, you and I cannot produce "success" any more than a rock can produce water (Exodus 17:1-16, Numbers 20:1-13)—we need the LORD's favor!

And yet we live our lives as if it all depends on us!

A shift in perspective about *where* our success truly comes from is the dose of wisdom we need to "desist."

"The blessing of the LORD makes rich, and toil adds nothing to it" (Proverbs 10:22 ESV).

32
The Word Jesus Wants to Describe Your Life

> *"For my yoke is easy, and my burden is light."*
> ***Matthew 11:30 ESV***

"*Easy.*"

That's not the word we've been trained to believe that Jesus wants for us. *Many many many* adherents to the faith *would* claim or *do* claim whether by spoken *words* or the *lifestyle* they lead in the name of faith (not in Jesus' Name!) that the word is actually "*hard.*"

Their theology silently whispers that God is most pleased when things are *hard* for us.

For how can we learn to trust Him, they *reason*, unless things become hard for us? But let me ask you—is that how a father thinks of his children? Is that a father's hope for the little ones he loves? Is that how a father teaches trust? By making things *hard* on their child?

Consequences are necessary, to be sure, but what's with this image of God as someone who is always trying to teach us a lesson? No place for enjoyment—always trying to spoil our plans. That kind of living actually agrees with a foreboding spirit in the name of faith!

My point is this—while trials are definitely a time for us to grow in our faith—God's ultimate desire isn't for us to constantly be going through hardships or living a *hard* life. That would be like God never wanting the Israelites to go to the Promised Land (Joshua 3:1-17).

So perhaps you are on the banks of a Jordan River in your own life.

As you look back, you can see desert—sometimes for miles and miles (or years and years). So much so, in fact, that the landscape behind you threatens to define your expectations of what's in front of you. No matter how "promising" that land looks, the geography that you've come from can easily make you doubt not only the best ahead, but also God's heart.

"Easy" is probably not the word you'd chose to describe your expectation of the days ahead...

But what if that changed?

What if the *Promised Land* became your *expectation* instead of more *desert*?

What if you took Jesus at His Word—His one simple word? *EASY*.

Allow God Himself to confirm if He is speaking that word to your heart. But never make the mistake of allowing your *yesterdays* to define your *tomorrows*.

The most important question is, "What is God *currently* saying?"

I hear Him saying the most beautiful and welcome word: *Easy*.

33
God Is Able

"And God is able to make all grace abound to you..."
2 Corinthians 9:7 ESV

Let this be written over your day: *GOD IS ABLE.*

He's not just able to do powerful things in the *world* or save *someone* on the other side of the planet. He is able to do something in *your* life.

And that *something* which He is able to do is the *one thing* that you will need if you desire your life to be everything that God designed for you: *GRACE.*

You don't have to fight for it or strive for it. You don't have to "make something happen." You simply need to rest in the fact of the good news—God is able.

He is able, and I am grateful. I'm grateful that I don't inherit anything because of my self-effort, initiative, striving, or laboring. I inherit based on His grace in my life. And the best news of all? This verse says that God is able to make it *abound* in my life (2 Corinthians 9:7 ESV).

With this word over my life, I am excited for the days ahead because they are going to *abound* with God's *grace.* I believe He is able!

34

Wanting What You Have

"But godliness with contentment is great gain."
1 Timothy 6:6 ESV

We often have it backwards. We want what we *don't* have and forget about what we *do* have. We think that *this* is the way to have *gain.*

But what a wearisome road! The whole lot of it is caught up in striving to get more. The problem? Everything that you toil for to *obtain* will require the same amount of effort to *maintain.*

Not so in the Kingdom of God. As is often the case, we see the opposite of what you'd expect. This invisible reality where the "last are first" (Matthew 20:16) operates under this equally wonderful principle: Godliness with contentment *is* great *gain* (1 Timothy 6:6 ESV).

In other words, contrary to what we've been taught by the world and what we often fall into, the way to have great gain in your life is to be content with what you already have!

Another way of saying it would be: Want what you have and forget about what you don't!

That doesn't mean that you no longer have desires or purpose, effort, planning, or production. It doesn't mean that you ignore passion or throw godly desires to the wind. Not at all!

It means that our primary focus is to become a godly people who *learn how to want what we already have*! And in conjunction with the operation of the spiritual Kingdom, this doesn't come naturally.

If left to yourself you will be swept up in the world's efforts to "make a name for yourself" (Genesis 11:4). But godliness and contentment are *supernatural*—available to the children of the King who will chose to make Him their delight and learn how to want what they already have.

We live in a world surrounded by people who are always trying to gain and yet never satisfied (Proverbs 27:20), but we are true children who know that real gain is godliness with contentment!

Let us realign with that reality today!

35
One Thing

"...but one thing is necessary." ***Luke 10:42 ESV***

One thing.

Only one thing? Yes. But then, why do we often miss it? Is it because there are too many "other things" on my list? Or is it because the "one thing" is actually a "He" and that idea seems too abstract? Or do I make complex what is supposed to be simple?

Whatever the reason, the diagnosis in this passage is that Martha was "distracted" (Luke 10:40).

That word "distracted" has the idea that we are not able to focus on one thing at a time and that we are uncollected and disordered in our thinking.

God, help us be fully *alive* today, not distracted or drawn away from You by being over-occupied by the "many" instead of the "One."

36
Receive the Waiting

> *"The Lord is not slow to fulfill His promise as some count slowness, but is patient toward you..."* **2 Peter 3:9 ESV**

God often does His best work in slowness and stillness. But He is not slow according to our standards or reasons of slow. He is *patient.*

Many have received a promise from God in their hearts and then wondered as the time passed, was that really Him? They *reason*, either it was Him and He's just taking a long time, or it was not Him at all. But time is never an issue for God.

God's waiting is an act of grace toward us. He is doing things behind the scenes that we could never figure out or get done (let alone understand) on our own. What is our job then? When it appears that God's promise is "slow" in coming to pass we must do as this passage says—*count it* as patience!

1) Be grateful that God is not giving you something too soon that you could not maintain.

Just think of lottery winners who end up going bankrupt.

2) Stand firm in His promises.

We see from this passage that slowness is not an indicator of having misheard God. In fact, it seems to sometimes be confirmation in itself. The very fact that God *told us before it will happen* seems to indicate that it may be *some time* before it happens or that things are going to *appear* like it will not happen. Was that not true for all of God's examples in scripture who received and inherited promises? Was there not a period of waiting where it *appeared* as if the exact opposite of what was promised would happen? This is why our faith is one that walks without sight (2 Corinthians 5:7). We cling to things that are unseen (Hebrews 11:1).

3) Receive the waiting as a gift.

God is giving you the gift of the ability to wait longer then you think you should have to.

4) Do not give up.

"For you have need of endurance, so that when you have done the will of God you may receive what is promised" (Hebrews 10:36 ESV).

37
Judgment Without Mercy

"For judgment is without mercy to one who has shown no mercy." ***James 2:13 ESV***

Not judgment without *evidence*, for often we have plenty of evidence. Not judgment without *authority* because merely having authority over someone doesn't give way to open judgment. The judgment which will be met with equal heartless judgment is judgment without *mercy*.

Every decision we make about someone, their actions, and even our thoughts toward them must have mercy. Mercy triumphs over judgment (James 2:13).

The cold reality is that if we are harsh critics and endless cynics toward others, then that very same judgment will be shown toward us. We will forfeit the free flowing favor of the LORD in exchange for being harsh and heartless toward others.

You must be honest with yourself. Surely this kind of judgment which is spoken of above is not about the afterlife. It cannot be eternal judgment, for those who have embraced Christ are saved from that. This judgment then? It's the kind that's repaid now. The kind of judgment that makes you wonder how someone could be so heartless or careless. When you find yourself under the scrutiny of others, ask yourself, is this merely a byproduct of my own critical spirit?

Let mercy be your main focus today and you will experience that same freedom in your own life.

38
Draw Near

"Draw near to God and He will draw near to you."
James 4:8 ESV

It's an encouraging principle but one that I will only choose if I have true faith and don't fall for self-pity.

This verse would not be here if it was the *natural* thing to do. In other words, this is talking about doing something that you don't feel like doing—or else you would have already been doing it. And, another alternative is that you were simply unaware that this principle works whether you know about it or not.

The principle isn't that God only draws near to us if we do it first. No, for that would violate the character of God's *first love* we see throughout Scripture (1 John 4:19). This principle is simply that as creatures of free will, God does not ignore our *choice* to reach out to Him and draw near to Him. He promises to always draw near to us when we do that. And while this reaching out to Him is a choice we make, it is still only by His grace that we ever could or ever would.

Moreover, what a wonderful God we have knowing that we can call on Him whenever we desire and He promises to draw near!

As for this principle working even when we don't know about it, consider this. Perhaps there have been times where—because of my own independence, self initiative, and self will to try and solve a problem on my own—I missed His presence. Why? *Because I failed to draw near to Him.* Not because I had a bad heart or bad motives but perhaps because I was unaware that the very breakthrough I was trying to bring to pass on my own would have been the *easiest thing* when handed over to our loving God.

I desire to draw near. There are times where it can seem abstract. So instead of creating a system, I'll do the most simple way. I'll reach out to my God *with sincerity* and *wait* for Him to draw near.

39

Your Number One Priority

> *"But seek first the kingdom of God and His righteousness, and all these things will be added to you." **Matthew 6:33 ESV***

As a matter of first priority, importance, and placement, the Kingdom of God is supposed to rank *number one* in our lives.

But the honest ones among us will confess that our motives to make God our *priority* often don't match our motivation. We can have the best intentions in the world, but so many things often take the place of number one.

What am I seeking first?

Even when it's not recognition, success, provision, health, financial stability, relational contentment, or personal satisfaction—even when its not those things—am I not in great danger of allowing the most urgent fire dictate where my fountain goes? The worst part is that when you live your life putting out fires—the most urgent need of each moment —your fountain will eventually run dry.

We need the water welling up unto eternal life (John 4:14). We need the fountain of life (Psalm 36:9).

We need God to be *number one* to us—not just *theoretically* but in *actuality* and not just in our *hearts* but in our *practical daily lives.*

God, forgive me for relegating You to the end of my daily list, as if I could even make You a *task* to begin with. Forgive me for making You, time and time again, fall short of *number one* to me. May today be a turning point where I can truly say that I seek You first in my heart and in my daily life. Amen.

40

Honoring Those We Disagree With

> *"But I say to you, Love your enemies and pray for those who persecute you, so that you may be sons of your Father who is in heaven. For He makes His sun rise on the evil and on the good, and sends rain on the just and on the unjust."* ***Matthew 5:44-45 ESV***

One of the greatest marks of a secure son or daughter of God is the ability to support and honor someone who we do not agree with. This is quite simply because that is exactly what our Father does. And, if we are secure in Him and His love, we will do likewise.

It is amazing (in a pejorative sense) as to how many people the sons and daughters of God often reject, write off, or do not support who their Father in heaven actually does.

Somehow we have embraced a philosophy which says that if we honor or befriend someone who we believe is walking in error or who has done us harm in some way, we will somehow affirm them in that identity. It's almost as if we think that our kindness will solidify the very thing we disagree with.

But we see that the Father's rationale is the complete opposite. "Or do you presume on the riches of His kindness and forbearance and patience, not knowing that God's kindness is meant to lead you to repentance?" (Romans 2:4 ESV).

Showing *kindness* to someone and even *standing behind* someone is not the equivalent of standing behind *all* that they believe, say, think, or do. God sends rain and sunshine on the good and the bad (Matthew 5:44-45). He does not withhold good from those to whom it's due (Proverbs 3:27) and even gives to those to whom it is *not* due.

This has nothing to do with avoiding disagreements or not being clear about where you stand. This has everything to do with being fatherly toward people who have no father. And all children of true fathers know that their father will honor them and stand by them, even when the child is off track.

And I think we will find, when we feel that we need to make it a point to *not encourage* someone whom we disagree with, many times *our thinking* is off in some way.

Perhaps we are off in our *theology*, but *definitely* we are off in our *love*. For Jesus Himself tells us to do good and pray for those with whom we disagree or who have harmed us in some way.

God help us to be like You, our Father in Heaven, who makes it rain on the good and the bad. You are never afraid that they'll get the wrong message or somehow assume that your kindness means your complete agreement with everything they say, think, do, or believe.

41
A Life of Substance

"Now faith is the substance of things hoped for, the evidence of things not seen." **Hebrews 11:1 KJV**

Faith is the *substance.*

So if you want a life that has *substance* you must have a life of *faith.*

The word *substance* has deep meaning. The word we use in our modern language more frequently would be *conviction.*

A life of *substance* is living by *conviction.*

But conviction about what? Conviction about what you *cannot see.* It is the nature of faith to be about something that has not yet happened, not yet manifested, not yet been fulfilled. This, then, can be a tricky business because we usually base our convictions or certainty on things that we *can* see, touch, taste, or feel. But faith is more about *hearing* than any of the other senses. "So faith comes from hearing, and hearing through the word of Christ" (Romans 10:17 ESV). And, obviously I'm speaking of an internal kind of hearing. Just as Elijah was able to say, "I hear the sound of the rushing of rain" (1 Kings 18:41) long before the rain actually came (and following three and a half years of absolute drought)—*there is often a sound before a sight.* And we know that while our conviction may be strong, the sound itself could be as quiet as a whisper (1 Kings 19:12).

The simple fact remains—faith is about certainty, conviction, sureness of things that you *cannot see.* So here's my question: What is it that you are *sure* of these days? And not just that, but is there anything that you have a conviction about that has not yet come to pass?

One word of encouragement: That is not a sign of failure; that is a sign of faith.

When something is still in the waiting phase, we sometimes let our faith wane instead of recognizing that this is the very nature of faith itself! Don't lessen your sureness because of what you *cannot see*. Make sure you are hearing right and surrendered to God—and walk in total conviction. Your God is more than able to bring it to pass.

42
Then You Will Know

"Then you will know that I am the LORD; those who wait for me shall not be put to shame." ***Isaiah 49:23 ESV***

The promise is one of future fulfillment and it's encapsulated in a single word "then."

"Then" you will know that I am the LORD; those who wait for me shall not be put to shame (Isaiah 49:23 ESV). The "then" of this verse tells us that it is *yet to happen* but *certain to happen*. We can be sure that there is a specific moment in time for which we will know with certainty and unequivocal fulfillment, "It was all true, all of it."

"Then" or in *that specific moment*, we will have the full realization that every road of hardship we have gone down, every trial that has come our way, every tear we have cried, and every passing moment on the clock which has seemed to delay what we thought was so certain was all part of the story.

We often want *then* to be *now*, for that is how "thens" are realized. But they don't have to be realized before they are believed in.

When we start to have faith that our "then" is certain, our "nows" become moments of faith. And that kind of faith has real power to move any obstacles that are in our way (Matthew 17:20).

Do not doubt what the LORD has promised you just because today isn't "then." "Then" will come soon enough, and you will be able to jump for joy knowing that "not one word has failed of all the good promises He gave" (1 Kings 8:56).

43
Friends

"No longer do I call you servants, for the servant does not know what his master is doing; but I have called you friends, for all that I have heard from my Father I have made known to you." **John 15:15 ESV**

No longer *servants*. No longer *slaves*. No longer *orphans*.

Friends.

What's the difference? Well, a lot of things to be sure, but Jesus focused on one distinguishing difference: *Slaves don't know what their master is doing.*

What do slaves/servants/orphans know? Only what *they* are doing. It's a work of the flesh. Independence. Isolation. Strife.

The focus of slaves is their own tasks. Their daily lists. Their "doing over being."

But *friends* are focused on what God is up to. Their attention and thoughts are aware of His actions, thoughts, promises, heart, and ability. Only when we see God as our *friend* can we enter into true co-laboring with Him. This beautiful relationship is made possible by what Jesus has done for us on the cross because of God's great love and grace. And only then can we be free from the curse of the flesh called striving.

We find out so clearly here that Jesus didn't hide anything from us. He didn't consider us too low in rank to have the inside information. In the Kingdom of God their are no inside jokes making you feel outside of the group. Jesus discloses all that He would to us as a friend.

Of course, He leaves room for mystery and doesn't explain everything to us. But He never hides His true thoughts from us as one would do to an employee. We are co-owners of the business, so to speak.

Thank You, God, that You are a *Father* and *not a slave master*. You are a *Friend* and *not a boss*. You are our *Greatest* and *Best Companion*. Praise be to Your holy Name!

44
A Quiet Life

"Make it your ambition to lead a quiet life."
1 Thessalonians 4:11

Please note: It doesn't say, "Make it your ambition to lead a *busy* life."

Quietness is not your enemy.

Bored is the new black.

So much of our lives can be sidetracked if we feel that we must always be *doing* and that our doing must always *accomplish*. When we try to constantly accomplish great things we end up accomplishing nothing at all except burnout, defeat, and the like.

It was David who said "O LORD, my heart is not lifted up; my eyes are not raised too high; I do not occupy myself with things too great and too marvelous for me" (Psalm 131:1 ESV).

Our society tends to raise children as if they believe boredom is an enemy. This creates a constant dissatisfaction in our souls—setting the expectation for constant *doing*.

But the Biblical aspiration? A *quiet* life.

Quiet doesn't mean unproductive or meaningless. The meaning of this aspiration becomes clear when you contrast it with the opposite: A *loud* life.

Are you aspiring to live a *quiet* life or a *loud* one? You can find out today by simply watching your demeanor, stress level, activity, and ambition.

God, help us desire and pursue a quiet life! Amen!

45

Let Jesus Open the Door

> *"And to the angel of the church in Philadelphia write: 'The words of the holy one, the true one, who has the key of David, who opens and no one will shut, who shuts and no one opens.'"* ***Revelation 3:7 ESV***

Jesus opens doors that no one can close and closes doors that no one can open.

The great question of my days then is this: What doors am I trying to pry open that He has clearly shut? What doors am I trying to shut that He has clearly opened?

The most futile thing in our life is trying to open doors which have been sealed by God.

In fact, I am not called to try to open or close doors at all.

What is my calling? To walk through the doors that He opens.

Simply put, am I aware of the doors He has opened before me? Or am I more focused on my plan, my way, my door?

I'm not sure if the "no one" in this verse implicates us as well. It's unclear if we can force our way into a door that He has shut. I have found myself in many self-made catastrophes where God had clearly said "no." I remember once praying the most foolish prayer of my life and asking God to bring something about *even if it was against His will*!

At least my prayer was genuine—in that moment, I cared less about *His will* and more about *my plans*. But ultimately, His way proved best, and I learned one of the most valuable lessons of my life: *Never try to open doors that God wants closed.*

If His favor is on you, He can open doors that you would have never even been able to knock on, let alone open.

May the Great Door Opener, Jesus Christ, so clearly lead us to the doors that He has already opened. May our focus be upon Him and His clear path for us, and may we be grateful that He has called us to the simple task of walking through the open door.

46
The Condition of Possibility

"And Jesus said to him, '"If you can!" All things are possible for one who believes.'" **Mark 9:23 ESV**

You do not need to concern yourself with *how*. You only need to focus on *Who*.

The *Who* is the reason, after all, that you even have a chance of seeing the *impossible* become *possible.*

"If you can" comes from thinking about "how." *How* could it ever happen? Look at the odds! It's been *this* long, I just don't know how things will *ever* change.

But real faith requires simple focus on a *Who.* When our focus and trust is in Him, that's called believing. Jesus in the above passage says that *everything* is possible for the person who *believes.* The *Who* takes care of the *how.*

Has your *how* stolen your *Who*? Have you become so entrenched on how impossible things appear that you have forgotten you serve the *God* of the impossible?

You cannot make it happen. And every time you try to force your way, it is an indication that you have switched your focus back to "how."

Lose yourself in simple delight with *The Who* who graciously takes all responsibility for the *how* upon Himself. For after all, Jesus said that it's only when we lose our life that we will find it (Matthew 10:39). Perhaps we have made *responsibility* our god. We think we must do all these certain things to make sure our destiny is taken care of. When in reality, the opposite is true. Our true destiny is found by letting go in trust to the only *Who* who knows how. Leave the *how* to Him, and enjoy the wonder of *Who* He is.

God, would you move on our behalf today? We don't care *how* you do it—may our focus be on You. We declare and believe: *You are able!*

47
Your Expectations Matter

"Then He touched their eyes, saying, 'According to your faith be it done to you.'" ***Matthew 9:29 ESV***

Have you ever noticed that how you *think* it's going to go is often how it *does* go? Perhaps this is not prophetic insight as much as where you choose to place your faith.

I have witnessed countless times over the years where someone's anticipation (including negative anticipation) comes to fruition.

Negative faith is called foreboding and it's a demonic practice (Romans 1:21 KJV).

Obviously we cannot manufacture situations or have faith in our faith. Not at all! But shouldn't we have faith in God's *good plans* for us (Jeremiah 29:11) and *His ability* to work things together for our good (Romans 8:28)? Shouldn't we, therefore, stop foreboding the worst and start expecting the best?!

Truly, if we hope to live a life in the arms of God's great love, we will *always* believe the best (1 Corinthians 13:7).

That means staying in the moment and having hope about the future, not dread. There should never be a time where we allow our minds to ruminate over all that could go wrong. I believe that is an invitation for the enemy to carry out our fears. Does not anger manifest? Does not lust manifest? Then cannot fear manifest?

Your expectation of the best or the worst says a lot more about your *heart* than about your *circumstances*. Even more, it says volumes about your view of the character and nature of God.

“All the days of the desponding and afflicted are made evil [by anxious thoughts and forebodings], but he who has a glad heart has a continual feast [regardless of circumstances]” (Proverbs 15:15 AMPC).

“When a man is gloomy, everything seems to go wrong; when he is cheerful, everything seems right!” (Proverbs 15:15 TLB).

48
Forgotten by Man

"The chief cupbearer, however, did not remember Joseph; he forgot him." ***Genesis 40:23***

Forgotten again by man.

No matter. After Joseph had been betrayed by his brothers (Genesis 37:12-36), falsely accused by Potiphar's wife (Genesis 39:1-18), and thrown into prison for doing nothing wrong (Genesis 39:19-20), this seemed like the end.

But God's plan could not be stopped.

Joseph's destiny was secure, even if he was forgotten by man —betrayed nonetheless.

If only he could have known that it was all about to change in the very next verse. Of course, as must have been necessary, that one verse took two whole years to come to pass.

Two whole years (Genesis 41:1).

But once Joseph was delivered into his destiny, he was sure to be grateful for every part of his journey. So much so that he even later recognized that if his brothers had not betrayed him, a whole nation may have perished (Genesis 45:7-8).

Yes, let God work the pieces of your story together. Don't try to take the brush from His hands, for He is creating a masterpiece—however long and tedious it may seem in the moment, don't grow weary. Perhaps it will all change in the very next verse for you.

49
Don't Labor in Vain

> *"Unless the LORD builds the house, those who build it labor in vain. Unless the LORD watches over the city, the watchman stays awake in vain."* **Psalm 127:1 ESV**

I'm willing to build, LORD God, I am. But only at Thy *command.*

I'm willing to stay awake, LORD God, I am. But only by Thy *leading.*

I'm willing to do Your will, only if You'll *work through me*, and *go ahead of me* and *behind me*. But mostly *be near to me, be clear to me*. May I not live any of my days in vain.

And as it stands, when I don't see the progress I desire in a day, when I don't feel that I am hearing clearly, when I'm risking building or staying awake in vain—what else can I do but trust You? I'll trust that You have given me all I've needed for this day (Matthew 6:11). I'll trust that You don't want me to drag tomorrow's plans into today (Matthew 6:34). I'll trust that when—in the course of timing, events, and Your sovereign will—You should want me to pick up hammer and nails or rise while it is yet dark, You will indeed make it clear.

So in the meantime, I'll sleep. I'll rest in You. I dare not build what could only be called *vanity*, for that is not Your will. I'll wait for the next verse, the next day, the next instructions, and I'll learn to enjoy the slowness of *now*.

Perhaps tomorrow or even in the night, You will bring the breakthrough of clarity and direction I long for. And even if not, I dare not build. I dare not build monuments of my own creation (Genesis 11:4). I'll honor You in the waiting.

50
The Source of Disorder

> *"For where jealousy and selfish ambition exist, there will be disorder and every vile practice."* ***James 3:16 ESV***

Jealousy is hard to detect in yourself. It's elusive, because that is its very nature. We may be very jealous of an individual but the language we use in our minds to describe it are things like "unfair" or "disrespected" or "taken advantage of" or "mistreated" or "overlooked." Many more words could be words that we use to overshadow the truth that we are really *jealous* of that person—of their opportunity, of their situation, of their promotion, of their current life situation. Not to say that there aren't legitimate times where we are treated unfairly or taken advantage of—those do exist. And our every response should be guided by the Holy Spirit. Unfortunately, walking in jealousy absolutely prevents us from being Spirit-led. It's not only *not* a *fruit* of the Spirit, it *grieves* the Spirit (Ephesians 4:30). We cannot walk in jealousy and love at the same time. We cannot walk in our destiny while walking in jealousy.

Jealousy really goes back to what we believe about God and what we think God thinks of us. Jealousy is the ultimate volcanic eruption of ingratitude and discontentment. An ungrateful person will begin to leak bitterness the same way an infected wound will begin to leak pus. Bitterness is the natural byproduct of a jealous person. And that jealousy cannot be removed unless someone purposely chooses a grateful heart.

God does not force someone to be thankful; however, He refuses to let His children live as spoiled and ungrateful. Often, God allows us to go through situations which will expose our hearts. Hopefully, the jealousy we see is so repugnant to us that we quickly repent and turn back to God with gratitude for all that He *is* doing instead of discontentment about what He's *not* doing and especially without jealousy about what He's doing for someone *else*.

This verse in James is so powerful because it's a constant check when things fall apart. It literally tells us that when there is rivalry and jealousy and envy and self-promotion, *things will fall apart*. There will be disorder (James 3:16 ESV). Why is that? I don't know, but I can think of two reasons:

1) You are inviting the enemy in whenever you begin to think like he thinks.

Remember—Satan had everything, yet *failed to be grateful*. And out of *jealousy,* he wanted to take God's very high position.

2) God refuses to bless any work of the flesh.

Anything done out of jealousy or to promote yourself is simply a work of the flesh.

Jesus Himself said, "It is the Spirit who gives life; the flesh is no help at all. The words that I have spoken to you are spirit and life" (John 6:63 ESV).

It's very important to note also that it is God's *grace* to let something fall apart when it's a work of the flesh—born out of jealousy, rivalry, or selfish ambition. It's His *grace* to let it completely fail. He would rather us have the temporary pain of failure than the hell of a life spent living as someone who always has to make sure that they aren't taken advantage of and get put first in every way. He *spares us* from the hell of living like we are children without a Father and from the torment of feeling like if we don't promote ourselves, no one will notice. God is a gracious, loving Father. We should follow Jesus' example and stop clinging to what we *deserve* (Philippians 2:6) and start rejoicing for what we have been *given*. It's a very *heavenly* thing to consciously choose to focus on and be grateful for what you *have* instead of letting your mind slip off into the evil of focusing on what you *don't* have.

51
God's View of Himself

"The LORD passed before him and proclaimed, 'The LORD, the LORD, a God merciful and gracious, slow to anger, and abounding in steadfast love and faithfulness.'" **Exodus 34:6 ESV**

It's so comforting to know that this is how the LORD views Himself. He actually speaks in the third person about Himself saying that He is *gracious*, *slow to anger*, *abounding in steadfast love*, and *abounding in faithfulness*.

Just like the game of telephone, the farther down the line you get, the more distorted the representation can be of the original. Truth be told, it's often like this with God. Those who claim to represent Him don't always seem to have the same clarity about these things that the LORD does about Himself. So go to the Source.

And it's most important that we take Him at His Word about who He is. We must start to shape our views of God, His character, and His nature from the purity of the truest and best self-understanding there could be: God Himself.

So ask yourself:

In the midst of your prayers, do you believe that God is gracious?

In the midst of your mess-ups, do you believe that God is slow to anger?

In the midst of your relationships, do you believe that God abounds with love for you?

In the midst of your circumstances, do you believe that God abounds in faithfulness?

52
One Clarifying Question

> *"So now faith, hope, and love abide, these three; but the greatest of these is love."* ***1 Corinthians 13:13 ESV***

If you are confused about what to do in a certain situation, ask yourself: *What would love do?*

Many times passion can stir us to action, and that's not always a bad thing, but passion *becomes* a bad thing if it is rooted in the wrong things. For example, we can be passionately jealous, passionately angry, passionately selfish, passionately self-promoting, or passionately judgmental (sometimes mislabeled as "righteous indignation"). So may we not look to the level of our *passion* but the level of our *love.*

Another way of saying it is this: What is your motivation?

See, if your motivation isn't *love,* then it's not the *best* motivation. It doesn't mean that it's wrong, it just means that it's not the *best* motivation.

We see in the above verse that even between faith, hope, and love—three *great* things—the *greatest* is love.

So ask yourself that question. What would love do? Is my motivation truly love? We can look at all sorts of reasonings as to why we *should* do something, but I think it bears reflection, what *would* love do? Anything short of love doesn't mean it's bad, it means it's not the greatest possible motivation you could have.

Don't be led by *passion* or even by what you think is *clever*. The truth is that we must be led by the *Spirit* at all times (Romans 8:14). It is no coincidence the order in which Paul so eloquently pens the qualities that are birthed in the life of a person who is led by the Spirit: "But the fruit of the Spirit is love, joy, peace, patience, kindness, goodness, faithfulness, gentleness, self-control; against such things there is no law" (Galatians 5:22-23 ESV).

Love is *first* for a reason. May it be *our first* and highest priority and motivation. May we never trade the love that *God has for us* or the love that *He has given us for others* for any lesser thing.

God, please help my motivation be *love* today in all that I do. Amen.

53
How Long?

> *"How long, O LORD? Will You forget me forever? How long will You hide Your face from me? How long must I take counsel in my soul and have sorrow in my heart all the day? How long shall my enemy be exalted over me?"* **Psalm 13:1-2 ESV**

It should be pointed out that this was written by King David. That should be very encouraging in light of where he later ended up and the victory that God gave him.

Sometimes we have to pass through periods of seemingly insignificant waiting with no foreseeable progress to get to where God wants to take us. There are times where I'm not sure we can make any sense of it in the moment.

David himself was very honest and penned the words that many of us have at least *felt* before in our souls: *Have you forgotten me, God?*

Clearly, there was a temporary gap between what David *expected* to happen and his *current reality*. Bear in mind that—eventually—all that David expected and more came to pass. He became the king and was given even *more* than he desired (2 Samuel 12:8). But it came *later* than he wanted. Sometimes we trade fullness for fastness. We want the breakthrough now, but by getting it early, we get less of it—that is, if God's will is for us to wait. Just ask Abraham about trying to force his destiny into existence. The consequences of that are still felt to this day (Galatians 4:29).

David goes on to ask a question which is so deep, it's quite moving: *How long must I take counsel in my soul*? (Psalm 13:2 ESV).

He may be saying *many* things here but certainly we see a man who is making his plans but not seeing fruit. He is trying his best but not feeling full. He is doing everything he knows within himself to do, but it just isn't working. And he's simply wondering...*how long*?

How long do I have to try to figure this all out myself?

How long do I have to run scenarios in my mind of how You might bring the breakthrough, only to be proven wrong every time?

How long do I have to keep getting my hopes squashed?

How long will I have to continue with the appearance that I have been defeated, or at least, relegated to lesser than I thought You had promised?

And most of all, how long do I have to go it alone, feeling like I don't have a word from You, so I must counsel myself inside of my head?

How long? How long? How long?

It's a good question. It's a fair question. But it's a question, I think, that *must be asked* if it exists within us. For how can we *go forward* in our destiny if we are not truly honest with the LORD *right now*?

I think it's a question, that if asked with the right heart and in a reverent way, has the potential to free us from the very trap itself—the trap of feeling as if it's all on us to figure out and that there's no voice to be heard except our own reverberating off the walls of our soul.

We may not get an answer about timing. Sometimes we are not supposed to know (Acts 1:7). However, getting the answer is not always the reason we ask the question. Sometimes, we need to hear ourselves communicate what's going on deep within us to the LORD. Sometimes, we need to reach out with integrity of heart, laying out our true selves in complete surrender before the LORD. And, as He has promised, we can receive the *healing* that comes with such an appeal.

"For 'everyone who calls on the name of the Lord will be saved'" (Romans 10:13 ESV).

54
God Laughs

"He who sits in the heavens laughs." **Psalm 2:4 ESV**

It's nice to know that God has a sense of humor. Of course He laughs, for He created laughter.

He sits and laughs.

Amazing, though, the remarkably *light* side in which God places things that seem so *heavy* to us. What is He laughing at? He's laughing at the enemy's attempts to foil His plans, frustrate His people, and derail our destiny. God *laughs* at that.

Why, might I ask you, do you think God finds this so funny?

Is it not because of the great context He has of the enormous —no catastrophically unequal—power comparison which is going on? Is it not the equivalent of bringing a water pistol to a volcano? God is not in a power struggle with Satan—there is no comparison!

And yet, when we let every attempt of the enemy to disrupt our daily lives, frustrate us or cause us fear, anxiety, discouragement or depression, we respond totally unlike God does—He *laughs*.

May we begin to find humorous what He finds humorous. May we begin to see things in light of His majesty, abilities, and power. May we begin to be a people who are not moved by the threats of the enemy or the pressure of our circumstances. May we join with our Great God in Heaven in the cosmic comedy that He is witnessing of the gargantuan mismatch so ensuing.

Where we used to cry, may we laugh.

Where we used to fear, may we laugh.

Where we used to run, may we laugh.

And possibly where we used to pray prayers tossed up as an orphan-hearted desperate plea, may we instead join hearts with God by sitting down and having a good laugh.

He reigns! May our living be in light of His power and ability.

55
Easy to Please

"Whoever comes to me I will never drive away." ***John 6:37***

We can take Jesus at His word. He will *never* drive away someone who comes to Him. It is *never* His intention to make you turn away, run away, walk away, or give up on Him.

He *never* desires to make you trip up or fall. He is not looking to offend you (Matthew 11:6).

We have a merciful Savior who is also very relational. He doesn't turn away a single person who comes to Him!

What does this mean in light of your day? Your week?

Sometimes we can get into the habit of living as if Jesus is hard to please or at very best, standoffish. This couldn't be further from the truth! The times when we've drawn near to seek Him have never been wasted or in vain. When we cannot perceive His answer, it does not mean He is angry or done with us. We never have to approach Him halfheartedly. He is fully receptive every time we come.

Just imagine if there were a friend who was like that—never in a bad mood. Always happy to see you. Jumping for joy and elated that you would come. That would be someone who would be a delight to be around—and so it is with Jesus. His smile never fades and He never has a sudden turn of anger or short-tempered nature. He will not cast you away. He will not reject you. You can be 100% certain that *any time* you come to Him, He will always accept you.

It strikes me as noteworthy that one of the biggest things we are searching for in life (whether knowingly or unknowingly) is *total acceptance*. We want someone to accept us wholly and not reject us or brush us off. Some of the most hurtful times in our lives have been at the hands of another person who has rejected us and not treated us fairly or lovingly. But not so with Jesus!

He will never, in no way reject you or cast you out. Take heart today! "There is a friend that sticks closer than a brother" (Proverbs 18:24), and His Name is Jesus!

56

What Determines Your Destiny?

> *"...and calls those things which are not as though they were."* ***Romans 4:17 KJV***

It doesn't take a spiritual person to call things as they *are*. It merely takes a person with physical senses to take the temperature of a situation or circumstance.

But the spiritual realm is where things must shift *before you see* a breakthrough in your circumstances. We are not told to call things as they *are*. We are told to call things as God calls them—and He is in the business of calling things that are *not* as though they *are*.

What does this mean? It means that we can take any promise from Him to the bank, but we must begin writing checks before we see the actual cash. In this way, we are walking by *faith* and not by *sight* (2 Corinthians 5:7).

Faith clings to things *unseen* (2 Corinthians 4:18).

Faith is the conviction of things *not seen* (Hebrews 11:1).

So we see that we are called to walk by God-given *conviction* if we want to walk by *faith*.

To go even deeper, the truth is that much of what God wants to do in our lives is through the channel of faith, and if all we are doing is being "diagnosers" of the hardships, problems, history, and disappointments around us—we are living with a chain tied to us and our past experiences. Without faith, all we have to offer (or say about a situation) is what has already happened before and what is currently going on now. Let me remind you, it takes *no faith* to talk about how *bad* a situation is, how *unfair* a person was, how *unlikely* it is to work out for you, or how things are *currently going*. Any human being can talk about the past or the present without faith.

It reminds me of the verse: "You have circled this mountain long enough" (Deuteronomy 2:3 NASB).

Eventually, the song "she'll be coming around this mountain when she comes" should lead us to ask, "why is she still going around that mountain?"

In other words, how long will we look at the situation around us and continue to *accept more of the same* without evaluating *how we are relating* to that situation? What lies are we believing about God due to the circumstances which surround us? Surely something must be off if we keep on circling the same mountain and all we can focus on is what someone did to us ten laps ago.

How long will we continue to allow the disappointments of the past be our high-water mark for the future?

We are at least in danger of setting our expectations and hopes *so low* that we won't have to be disappointed again. But I'm telling you, when we live this way, we will always speak about things without hope, in light of the past instead of God's plan for our future. But with faith, we will believe what God has *said* over how we *feel* or what we have *experienced*.

We will believe His Word and the conviction in our hearts which He has placed there. We will believe God for what He's about to do. We will believe that He is a good God (Psalm 34:8) with an extraordinary plan and future for us (Jeremiah 29:11). We will believe that He is a good Father (Matthew

7:11), He never gives bad gifts to His children (James 1:17), and He's absolutely interested in fulfilling the healthy desires of our hearts (Psalm 37:4).

I think that Satan carefully crafts a plan to get us to stop believing the stuff above because of how things have gone *before*. Then, we place our hope—not in our *Great God*—but in the *past*. Which makes us stuck in the past, or at least, stuck in a rut. Then, we begin to spew out those lies: "It will always be this way." "Things will never change." "This always happens to me." "I'll never see it come to pass." "Great things never happen for me." When these become your pattern of speech, then guess what? The second you make those declarations, you have automatically welcomed more of the same into your life.

Why?

Because we are echoing the heartbeat of the enemy—we are coming into agreement with his lies. Are these things not obviously anti-Biblical to utter? And yet, how we *feel* sometimes trumps what we *claim to believe* about the authority of God's Word. And so it goes. Circling *round the mountain*, when the breakthrough could have been *just around the corner*, or in a more real sense, *just at the tip of your tongue* where the power of life and death reside (Proverbs 18:21).

Don't make the mistake of allowing your circumstances, your past, or your feelings to determine your destiny. Don't allow those things to make you stumble into agreement with the enemy of your soul. Instead, turn it around. Start claiming what God says through His Word (Hebrews 4:12). Start proclaiming the *sureness* you have about what He is promising you (Hebrews 11:1), and guess what? You will begin to align yourself with Almighty God, whose main way of creating is "calling things that are not as though they are" (Romans 4:17). Is it not true that God Himself operates in this way?

"By faith we understand that the universe was created by the word of God, so that what is seen was not made out of things that are visible" (Hebrews 11:3 ESV).

So the question is, what are you allowing to become the focus of your thoughts *and* the expression of your words—what is *seen* or what is *unseen*?

May I remind you, "The things that are seen are transient, but the things that are unseen are eternal" (2 Corinthians 4:18 ESV).

Start walking in the eternal power of our good and loving Father today by speaking life instead of death and taking a clear stand upon the Word of God. It will *always* trump your circumstances, your past, and your feelings—unless you walk just as any other man or woman can and live simply by what you *see*.

I have heard this from many sources over the years, but it's never been truer than today: Anyone can take the temperature of the room, but we are called to be thermostats. Start setting the temperature instead of merely measuring it.

57
Don't Try to Force It

"It may be that the LORD will work for us, for nothing can hinder the LORD from saving by many or by few." ***1 Samuel 14:6 ESV***

Faith will often require risk. This means "stepping out" in line with what we are certain God has shown, but not sure of all the *details*.

Faith walks by conviction (Hebrews 11:1), but conviction is not the same thing as having an instruction manual. We don't always have everything laid out before us ahead of time. Sometimes, we simply take things step by step in faith.

The best part of it all is that nothing can hinder the LORD from working on our behalf. Why? Because He is not *restrained* to save by many or by few (1 Samuel 14:6).

In the context of this passage it meant that God wasn't forced into a box to save people by using a *big* army, and neither was He forced into a box to save people by a *small* army.

Translation: God can do it the *easy* way or the *hard* way.

He's not restrained.

Sometimes we try to restrain Him or put Him in a box. We do this by either thinking that God can only bring the deliverance or breakthrough in a miraculous or impossible way (hard way). Or we think that God has to do it through normal, natural means or slowly over time (easy way).

Most often in faith, the conviction we have isn't about *how* He is going to move, it's just *that* He's going to move. And that is the most peaceful condition to stay in. Fully entrusting ourselves—our entire being—into His hands, regardless of *how* He chooses to move. That's His to figure out. Ours is to walk by faith—to follow Him and believe that "He will work for us" (1 Samuel 14:6).

The shortest route to disappointment is to operate not as a believer in God but as a believer in your *own plan* of how God should move. It's an easy line to cross. We have a conviction about something that God has promised us, and it's easy to immediately begin to plan how He wants it to come about. Sadly, this can even turn into us trying to *force* God to bring His promise to pass. It only takes a look at the life of Abraham to realize that it's ever so important to not try to force a promise into existence (Genesis 16).

So let's not put God in a box—assuming that He has to move a certain way, whether it's the *easy way* or the *hard way*. And may we never try to force God to fit our plan. Let Him be God!

"Do not stir up or awaken love until the appropriate time" (Song of Solomon 8:4 CSB).

58
An Extra Special Gift

> *"The Lord is not slow to fulfill His promise as some count slowness, but is patient toward you..."* ***2 Peter 3:9 ESV***
>
> *"Every good gift and every perfect gift is from above, coming down from the Father of lights, with whom there is no variation or shadow due to change."* ***James 1:17 ESV***

Sometimes God wants to give us, not only a *promise*, not only the *fulfillment* of the promise but an *extra special gift.*

That extra special gift is the *gift of the ability to wait longer than you think you should have to.*

At first glance, it does not seem like a gift you would want to open. However, once you receive the fulfillment of the promise in your life, you will realize that the gift of the ability to wait longer than you think you should have to is actually a "good and perfect gift" (James 1:17).

Why are we often afraid of this gift? Sometimes as Peter tells us, we are afraid that *slowness to answer* means that God is not going to do it after all. But that's not the case. It's actually His patience toward us—and His *timing* is part of preparing us to receive the fullness of all that He has planned. Sometimes we are afraid of this gift because we equivocate *waiting* with *wasted* time—as if being busy, regardless of if it is in line with our destiny, could ever bring fulfillment. But most of the time, we are afraid of this gift because we are *afraid of missing out*. We think that if we don't act now or do something to bring that promise to pass, then we will miss it. Deep down, we think that waiting is foolish.

But the best and most beautiful things come by waiting.

“See how the farmer waits” (James 5:7 ESV).

“Indeed, none who wait for You shall be put to shame…” (Psalm 25:3 ESV).

“Then you will know that I am the LORD; those who wait for me shall not be put to shame” (Isaiah 49:23 ESV).

Don’t be discouraged or confused. Embrace this beautiful gift from the LORD and receive with gladness the ability to wait longer than you think you should have to.

59
An Audience with God

"If I had cherished sin in my heart, the Lord would not have listened." ***Psalm 66:18***

What remains impure in me?

And, am I even concerned about it? Do I, like David, cry out for God to remove any patterns or thoughts of my old life from me? Do I yearn to be searched out by the Most High to find any secret sins in my life?

"Search me, O God, and know my heart! Try me and know my thoughts! And see if there be any grievous way in me, and lead me in the way everlasting!" (Psalm 139:23-24 ESV).

God does not want us to feel like failures or constantly be down on ourselves. Not at all! However, He desires for us to have a purity of heart and not cling to our old ways. This change happens first in our thought patterns and then is lived outward, often to our speech and then actions. So, if I have not changed my secret inner thought life, desires, and pleasures—I do not have a "transformed life" (Romans 12:2).

This is not something found in only the Old Testament. Ephesians 5:3 tells us that there is to not even be a "hint" of sexual immorality among believers. What's the implication? That cherishing the thought of sin is wrong. Not simply the *act of*, in this case, fornication or adultery, but the very *cherishing of* it in our hearts.

David believed this so strongly that he said there was a special audience with the LORD that he would have forfeited if he secretly cherished sin in his heart (Psalm 66:18). Is this not the same thing that Jesus said? "Blessed are the pure in heart, for they shall see God" (Matthew 5:8 ESV).

God, I want to have that special audience with You—I want to *see* You. Please search my heart and cleanse me of all impurity and the thoughts from the old me. I am a new creation in You (2 Corinthians 5:17), and I have the mind of Christ (1 Corinthians 2:16). May I live in line with who I truly am in You, and may I walk with a pure heart! In Jesus' Name, Amen!

60
Eat Up!

> *"Your words were found, and I ate them, and Your words became to me a joy and the delight of my heart, for I am called by Your name, O LORD, God of hosts."* ***Jeremiah 15:16 ESV***

Is God's Word precious to me?

What I believe will always manifest in my speech and actions. So, what am I *talking* about? What am I *doing*? Is my life truly shaped by His Word?

Is my day littered with all other things and yet missing something that is supposed to be *precious* to me?

I wonder, how often God has brought a word, and I refused to eat.

I wonder, how often have His words become a joy and delight to my heart?

I see how His Word can become "just another thing" to me instead of "a lamp to my feet and a light to my path" (Psalm 119:105 ESV).

I can recall the days when the *preciousness* of His Word drew me away from my self-initiative and self-made agenda and *watered my soul*. May it be so again LORD!

May God's Word not be brushed aside in my life today, or any day. May I hold it as *precious*, and as Jeremiah did, may I eat His very words today.

61

What Are You Sowing?

"A man reaps what he sows." **Galatians 6:7**

This is a spiritual principle which means it is working in the background of our lives even if we don't know about it. Principles don't work because you *believe them* to be true or *know about them* but because they are *principles*. Whatever you *sow* is what you will eventually *reap* (Galatians 6:7).

Truth be told, we are all, in some way, reaping what we have sown in past seasons. The planting of previous seasons in our lives is reaping a harvest now. Sometimes, that means *consequences* for cutting corners. Other times, it means a *reward* for our faithfulness.

We should keep in mind that what we are reaping right now may not be an indicator of current faithfulness but past sowing. So don't be discouraged if you have changed the seeds you are sowing but have continued to reap something different. Give it *time*, and the increase will come.

But most of all, let us focus not primarily on the *harvest* of our days but on what we are *sowing*. Perhaps *today* is not the day that the *harvest* of all of the hopes and dreams and acts of faith will be reaped, but it is another day *that we can sow* the right kinds of seeds for the next season in our lives.

What can you do today that will reap great rewards for your next season?

62
Addicted to Drama

> *"When Jesus saw him lying there and knew that he had already been there a long time, He said to him, 'Do you want to be healed?'"* ***John 5:6 ESV***

It is possible to be addicted to drama.

Problems, hard circumstances, being the underdog...for some strange twisted reason, some people can unknowingly embrace these as part of their core identity. In finding satisfaction by always having a problem to complain about or try to cure, these people welcome *more of the same* in their lives.

We must also be careful to not find entertainment in others' drama, bad circumstances, or problems.

There are some who get their highs out of recounting their problems. And if there wasn't a fire to put out, they wouldn't know what to do with themselves.

Since the Kingdom of Heaven is described as a situation where even the lion and the lamb lay down together (Isaiah 11:6), we may need to reevaluate whether or not we are walking in the true peace of God if we cannot *sit still.*

I'd like to suggest to you that constant problems, issues, and drama may be more of a product of personal values than demonic attacks.

Perhaps there is a reason that God sometimes has to "make us" lie down in green pastures (Psalm 23:2). Perhaps it's because we have become so accustomed to problems that we are afraid of what it's like to have *none*. Could this be why Jesus is asking the man in the above verse what should be a blatantly obvious answer?

"Do you want to be healed" implies that there are those (and perhaps even this man) who actually do *not*. Now don't get me wrong, it could be that the weight of their circumstances has driven them into *complacency*—relegated to accepting their situation as their permanent reality. But just remember, problems can become addictive.

We all know people who seem to always have drama going on in their lives. How is it that they don't know it? From the outside, we can see that they are caught up in the dramatic and problematic, but they themselves have not a clue.

May this be a wake up call to us as well. May we never value the problems of the day. May we never look upon time lying in a green pasture with the LORD as wasted (Psalm 23:2). In Heaven, there are no problems (Revelation 21:4). Let's follow Jesus' model of bringing Heaven to earth (Matthew 6:10) and not making our identity out to be someone who is always fighting fires. Instead, let us be people who have the favor of the LORD upon them and who have learned to enjoy true rest (Matthew 11:28).

63
Condemning Ourselves

> *"Therefore you have no excuse, O man, every one of you who judges. For in passing judgment on another you condemn yourself, because you, the judge, practice the very same things."* **Romans 2:1 ESV**

How convicting are God's words to us! The people who tick us off the most are the ones who are doing the very things we do. No way, you say. But take a closer look and you will find that we are *hardest* on the people who do things that we don't like about *ourselves*, whether now or in the past.

Here's what I mean. When we judge others—meaning we let judgment, critical thoughts, and condemnation trump mercy—it is always the case where part or all of what they are doing or have done can be found in our own hearts and lives, whether we are currently operating that way or we used to. Part of it can be so annoying because *they* haven't learned something that we *have*.

But I would like to suggest to you that if our tendency is to judge things in people who are like us, then we can turn the situation around. What if we became people who looked for things in others that we like about ourselves? What if we viewed people with the honor, integrity, and purity that we know God is developing in us? Wouldn't that actually be following, to some degree, the command of Christ to "love others as you love yourself" (Matthew 22:39)? The implication is that if we *hate ourselves* and trip over every fault we have—constantly judging and criticizing ourselves—we will have no capacity to love *others*. This is why being a fault-finder only makes *you* miserable!

And further, what if we, in finding a person to not measure up to the things we have learned (albeit through the painful processes we ourselves had to go through), actually extended mercy to them the way that we *wish others had* extended to us? What if we viewed them in light of how we would have liked to be treated (Matthew 7:12)?

It is counterintuitive and definitely not found in the realm of logic, but treating other people in light of the same mercy and grace we have received from God is an inescapable reality of the Kingdom of God (Ephesians 4:32).

May it be evident today as we look to be a people who allow *mercy* to triumph over *judgment* (James 2:13).

64
Charge!

"Such knowledge is too wonderful for me; it is high; I cannot attain it." ***Psalm 139:6 ESV***

There comes a point in our destiny where we have a revelation of the utter impossibility of its fulfillment unless God intervenes. We see clearly, perhaps for the first time in a while, the almost laughable disparity between *what needs done* and *what we have to offer*.

But deep faith becomes focused on God and His ability. We *do not* let the deficits and shortcomings in our own lives make us doubt or become discouraged. But we *do* change the way we approach that which is ahead of us. We do not, as the enemy would have it, lower our heads in defeat. Neither do we lower them with our nose to the grind, relying on our own will power or sheer effort of grit and endurance to win the battle. That would be foolish. After everything we've gone through, we all have had that lesson taught to us in some measure before. That's why Paul says to the Galatians who had fallen into self-effort: "Did you suffer so many things in vain—if indeed it was in vain?" (Galatians 3:4 ESV).

So instead, we raise our heads in all honesty and sincerity to the Only One who has the ability to fulfill His promise.

We no longer fool ourselves to think that we could somehow "figure it all out" or master some plan well enough that we could bring anything to pass. We *don't* give up, but we *do* surrender. We surrender to the God who has prophesied our destiny over us in times past (1 Timothy 1:18) and who also will not leave us as orphans (John 14:18).

But we *do* charge forward with confidence in the same God about whom David was able to unashamedly declare, "'You come to me with a sword and with a spear and with a javelin, but I come to you in the name of the LORD of hosts, the God of the armies of Israel, whom you have defied. This day the LORD will deliver you into my hand, and I will strike you down and cut off your head. And I will give the dead bodies of the host of the Philistines this day to the birds of the air and to the wild beasts of the earth, that all the earth may know that there is a God in Israel'" (1 Samuel 17:45-46 ESV).

So we walk in the footsteps of Abraham who "faced the fact that his body was as good as dead" (Romans 4:19) yet who "did not waver through unbelief regarding the promise of God, but was strengthened in his faith and gave glory to God" (Romans 4:20).

Yes, such knowledge *is* too wonderful for us. It is high, we cannot attain it (Psalm 139:6 ESV). And in light of that, we calm and quiet our souls, not getting involved in matters too great for us (Psalm 131:1-2). In this peaceful yet confident state, we shift the focus *off* of *our inability* and *on* to *His total ability* to fulfill that which He has promised.

"And God is able to make all grace abound to you, so that having all sufficiency in all things at all times, you may abound in every good work" (2 Corinthians 9:8 ESV).

65
The Road Less Traveled

"Do not put yourself forward in the king's presence."
Proverbs 25:6 ESV

What if doing something would cause your advancement so to speak and yet still not be God's will for you? Is the trade off worth it? So it is today in our culture where the end justifies the means and in doing so, obscures the end from God's plan of promotion for us.

"For promotion cometh neither from the east, nor from the west, nor from the south. But God is the judge: He putteth down one, and setteth up another" (Psalm 75:6-7 KJV).

We must be aware of the magnetic pull of the world toward self-promotion and recognize that though outwardly it promises our wellbeing, it will truly bring disorder, not only in our lives but in our very souls (James 3:16).

Jesus wasn't mincing words when He asked about the trade off. What would it profit a man if he gained the world yet forfeited his soul (Mark 8:36)? The very question proves that the possibility exists. It seems more of a question of motives that giants would face. But the reality is, it begins in the smallest decisions we face.

Will we seek our own advancement or seek *first* the Kingdom of God (Matthew 6:33)?

It may appear foolish to not jump at the opportunity to put yourself forward before the king, but in the end it will prove to be one of the wisest decisions you've ever made. And, the

King will call you up to a higher seat than the one you've taken.

"But when you are invited, go and sit in the lowest place, so that when your host comes he may say to you, 'Friend, move up higher.' Then you will be honored in the presence of all who sit at table with you" (Luke 14:10 ESV).

"Kings shall see and arise; princes, and they shall prostrate themselves; because of the LORD, who is faithful, the Holy One of Israel, who has chosen you" (Isaiah 49:7 ESV).

So what to do? Humble yourself under the mighty hand of God, and He will exalt you at the proper time (1 Peter 5:6).

Choose the road less traveled and watch how God will promote you. All you need to focus on is delighting yourself in Him (Psalm 37:4)!

66
Silence

"The LORD is good to those whose hope is in Him, to the one who seeks Him; It is good to wait quietly for the salvation of the LORD. It is good for a man to bear the yoke while he is young. Let him sit alone in silence." ***Lamentations 3:25-28 ESV***

"He giveth quietness." ***Job 34:29 KJV***

"For God alone my soul waits in silence; from Him comes my salvation." ***Psalm 62:1 ESV***

There's real power in silence. When I have found myself in situations which were pressing or times that were hard to bear, I can distinctly recall asking God, what do I have to offer in a situation like this? The revelation in those recalled times was simple: "I can offer my silence."

We are trained to think the best course in hard situations would be a grandiose speech or even a jarring sentence or two. But when faced with the imposition of pressing times, while having much I *could* say, I have found that I was able to inject peace into a room by my *silent trust* in God.

Don't get me wrong, there are many times when God calls us to speak and even gives us a word that cuts right to the heart. But the revelation we need right now is that we don't always have to give voice to what we are thinking—let alone how we are feeling. God gives us not only self-control but a sound mind (2 Timothy 1:7). But sometimes they come progressively. As I choose to *exercise* self control, my thoughts and feelings come in line with my core beliefs, and the truth sets free (John 8:32).

Isn't it true that there have been times where what you were *feeling* was not true and yet you gave voice to it and regretted it? Had you waited in silence, trusting in God alone for your salvation in the matter, all would have been made well. And while today is still called today (Hebrews 3:13), we have that chance.

"For God alone my soul waits in silence; from Him comes my salvation" (Psalm 62:1 ESV).

67
He Is Our Peace

> *"For He Himself is our peace, who has made us both one and has broken down in His flesh the dividing wall of hostility."* **Ephesians 2:14 ESV**

We miss the peace that God has for us when we think we will find it in anything other than Christ Himself. He actually is the peace we so desperately need.

We can brainstorm, plot, plan, and execute all we want, but until we recognize that Christ Himself is our peace, we will chase countless means to no end. We will search and not find. We will ask but not receive. We will knock with no answer. Why? Because we are knocking at the wrong door. We are knocking at the door of trying to find peace by self effort or achievement instead of what has *already been achieved* for us. What's that? Namely that the dividing wall of hostility has been torn down. Jesus did the work. Let's not try to tear down a wall that is no longer standing. The truth is, the work is done, God is near, and He Himself is our peace —currently in our possession—only masked by our relentless pursuit of it elsewhere.

Jesus, I confess, You Yourself are my peace, and I rest in You today knowing that I don't have to work anything up and that I can simply believe Your Word that it truly is "finished" (John 19:30).

68
Rejection

"Jesus said to them, 'Have you never read in the Scriptures: "The stone that the builders rejected has become the cornerstone; this was the Lord's doing, and it is marvelous in our eyes?"'" ***Matthew 21:42 ESV***

The builders seemed like *important* people. However, their authority must have been quite limited in scope, indeed, more than they even perceived. For if they had it their way, they would have never allowed the Stone to be the Corner—the most important and elevated and promoted place in a building. Without that Stone, all would crumble and there would be no gauge to build a straight or strong structure.

Jesus knows exactly what it's like to be rejected by the very ones He longed to be close with.

Perhaps rejection is even an indicator of one who has a destiny so grand that the enemy must already have caught wind of it.

Rejection is often the pathway to promotion.

The most peculiar phrase is "this is the Lord's doing" (Matthew 21:42 ESV). The most obvious question, then, is *what*? *What* is the Lord's doing? Certainly the exaltation. Certainly the most prominent placement of being the Cornerstone. But is there no hint here that God's sovereign will *included* rejection by man? What is so marvelous in their eyes? Could it be that they found it

marvelous that rejection by men was a necessary part on the road to promotion?
At some point we all must learn the lesson—that while we may be rejected by man, we are *never* rejected by God.

It could have been that very thought that allowed David to "strengthen himself in the LORD" when all his earthly friends abandoned him (1 Samuel 30:6). And so too, Jesus, when they struck the Shepherd and the sheep were scattered (Mark 14:27). But unlike man, God has promised to never leave us or forsake us (Joshua 1:5).

May we not forget this precious eternal truth when we find ourselves rejected by men. Keep in mind that the very people who rejected Jesus were the ones He died for—and so goes the story of the love of God. May you realize that rejection is not a sign of the end for you but a precipice, a marker, and an indicator of your incredible destiny and your loving God who will *never*—no *never*—forsake you (Hebrews 13:5).

"As you come to Him, a living stone rejected by men but in the sight of God chosen and precious" (1 Peter 2:6 ESV).

69
God's True Delight

"In sacrifice and offering You have not delighted, but You have given me an open ear. Burnt offering and sin offering You have not required." ***Psalm 40:6 ESV***

God's delight is not simply in our *giving* but in our *receiving*. We often believe that if we only do more, try harder, regroup, plan better, and put forth our all, it will produce fruit. But the most beautiful reality of the Gospel is that eternity starts *now*. Our relationship with God is one of receiving. It's not that we *don't* give. It's not that we *don't* make an offering. But those things *flow out of* this one thing: *Receive*.

"But to all who did receive Him, who believed in His name, He gave the right to become children of God" (John 1:12 ESV).

Psalm 40:6 draws a contrast. What are we substituting for the real thing and in so doing, missing that thing which delights God's heart? Are we trying to produce instead of receive?

We are busy with self-effort and self-initiative, and if we're honest, self-promotion. And before too long, there's so much "self" going on that we cannot hear God through all of the noise. The offerings and sacrifices can easily become all about self. But even more important, notice what God gives us instead: "An open ear" (Psalm 40:6 ESV).

What fools we have been to allow self-initiative to block out the very voice of the LORD which would have actually brought everything we've been longing for!

If self-made offering and sacrifice has plugged your ears, just think rationally for a moment: Would God want you to spend your whole life striving, trying to produce fruit on your own, or engaging in a *listening* relationship with Him?

Jesus has made the sacrifice. He has made the offering. But real sheep are not trying to go out and reproduce His finished work. Real sheep *hear* His voice (John 10:27). God does not want us out "baaing" around trying to turn our wool into clothes. He's perfectly content for us to stay in the pasture and wait for the moment when He clearly calls us to our next assignment. But even then, may we not run ahead of our Shepherd and live from a place of self-sufficiency and self-initiative. God is not looking for you to perform; He's looking for a listening ear.

"Therefore, while the promise of entering His rest still stands, let us fear lest any of you should seem to have failed to reach it" (Hebrews 4:1 ESV).

70
Faith Will Become Sight

"And the LORD said to Moses, 'Is the LORD's hand shortened? Now you shall see whether my word will come true for you or not.'" **Numbers 11:23 ESV**

Never envision your destiny based upon your own abilities. We often project upon others what we see in ourselves. The same can be true for our relationship with God. We sometimes measure the extent of our future based upon our current reality, ability, or experience.

Sometimes we view God in light of our own shortcomings—thus prompting God to ask the question: Has your view of *Me* become limited by your view of *you*? Do you really think that My hand is shortened or that I cannot save?

God wants us to have ultimate confidence in what He has *promised*—even over what we *see*. The great news is that one day your faith *will* become sight.

In this passage above, God tells Moses that the limitations people think He has are not true. There is nothing outside of God's power or ability. He's not like us—He has no shortcomings.

Then God tells Moses something that I find so soothing: *"Now you'll see"* (Numbers 11:23 ESV).

I'd love to know how soon the "now" of the LORD is. Maybe it is "right now" or "about now" which is more like "just around the corner." But either way, isn't the most important part of this whole thing the fact that *one day we will actually see it*? One day, there will be a moment in time where it all comes to pass, just as God said it would, and in that particular moment in time we will have the divine revelation: "Then you will know that I am the LORD; those who wait for me shall not be put to shame" (Isaiah 49:23 ESV).

I love how the Amplified Bible translates this verse: "And you shall know [with an understanding based on personal experience] that I am the Lord; For they shall not be put to shame who wait *and* hope expectantly for Me" (Isaiah 49:23 AMP).

With an understanding based on *personal experience*! That is so powerful!

It's clear that God wants us to have an understanding *prior to* and perhaps even *separate from* experience—not simply rooted in what we've experienced but in what He has said! Then, as we have faith, it will eventually become sight, and in that particular moment we will have *graduated* to have an "understanding based on personal experience" (Isaiah 49:23 AMP).

It's like when you put a seed into the ground. You believe it will grow a crop. But there are many days where the ground is just as barren or dry as before you even planted the seed. But then, one day, you come outside to witness the breakthrough in the ground—a sprout has formed, and a plant is growing. In that moment, your faith has become sight, and you reap the benefits of sowing an investment that was not based simply on what you saw.

Take note: God is in no way insecure about what He has promised you and neither should you be! God is not worried about *how* what He said will come to pass. All He's asking us to do is to believe—and with the kind of faith that brings great rest to the soul—sit back, relax, and enjoy the show!

"Now you shall see whether my word will come true for you or not" (Numbers 11:23 ESV).

"Also henceforth I am He; there is none who can deliver from my hand; I work, and who can turn it back?" (Isaiah 43:13 ESV).

Do not let your difficulty define your destiny. Instead, shift your focus solely upon God—His character, His nature, and His promises. What He has *proclaimed*, He will *perform*!

71
Our Elder Brother

> *"For those whom He foreknew He also predestined to be conformed to the image of His Son, in order that He might be the firstborn among many brothers."* **Romans 8:29 ESV**
>
> *"For He who sanctifies and those who are sanctified all have one source. That is why He is not ashamed to call them brothers."* **Hebrews 2:11 ESV**

There is no jealousy with Jesus even though He chooses to share His inheritance among countless brethren. Why is that the case?

Well, obviously, this is because He's God and His character does not have unrighteous jealousy or envy. We know that has to be the case because even His half brother James said, "For where jealousy and selfish ambition exist, there will be disorder and every vile practice" (James 3:13 ESV).

But alongside of that reality parallels another: There is no *lack* with God.

I've heard the example many times that when asked to share a pizza with his fellow brother, a man became increasingly jealous that his brother was eating more than his "fair share." That is, until that same man realized their father owned the entire pizzeria. He had an *unlimited supply* at his disposal, and yet he was focused on his rights to a single pizza!

Is this not like the elder brother of The Prodigal Son story who is bitter that his dad never gave him *a goat* until he realizes that he actually owns the *whole farm* (Luke 15:29-31)? His jealousy of his younger brother was not founded in reality because he had shaped his existence on a lie. He started to believe that areas of lack were his father's heart for him. He started to look at the people around him who were prospering—even within his own family—and thought that he deserved it more. But when push came to shove, his worldview of lack and disadvantage did not get him "his fair share"—it kept him *out of the party*. Oh how the father pleaded with that elder brother to just come into the party and stop worrying about what he felt he did not get (Luke 15:28)!

Yes, everything the father had belonged to that elder brother (Luke 15:31), but he didn't perceive how large his inheritance was—and it kept him in a state of constant bitterness, disappointment, and lack. He was completely focused on what other people had.

I am so thankful that Jesus is not an Elder Brother like that! He is a brother who is proud to be called the firstborn among *many* brethren (Romans 8:29 KJV). Those brethren or brothers are us! He is not threatened by *many* family members because He knows how to walk in the favor of His Father, and He understands something the elder brother of Luke 15 did not, *He owns the whole farm.*

God, please help us to not compare what we have or what we lack with the people around us. Break us out of a poverty mentality where all we know to do is focus on what we don't have. Give us the divine revelation, most precious, that *all You have belongs to us*. Thank you for sending Jesus to pay the price that we could not pay to win the reward that we do not deserve. Thank You that Jesus is not jealous or begrudging in His generosity. He has welcomed us to fully share in His inheritance (Romans 8:17)!

May I start living like that is true this very day, and may the lack that I perceive melt away before me as I start writing checks from the account that I never knew I had. In Jesus' Precious Name, Amen!

"As the deer panteth for the water
So my soul longeth after Thee
You alone are my heart's desire
And I long to worship Thee

You're my friend
And You are my brother
Even though You are a King
I love You more than any other
So much more than anything."

-*As the Deer*, Maranatha! Singers

72
Like Children

> *"Truly, I say to you, unless you turn and become like children, you will never enter the kingdom of heaven."* ***Matthew 18:3 ESV***

There is a general simplicity about children that we often mistake for immaturity. It cannot be immaturity which Jesus asks us to seek. But perhaps we have misunderstood what a mature man or woman in the LORD should actually look like.

When asked what it takes to be a mature Christian, pictures often come to mind of the staunch and serious individuals who have so developed their self-control that they are never even in danger of cracking a smile. But the image of a joy-filled, happy-go-lucky child rarely comes to mind. Why is that?

Why is it that we think children just "don't understand yet." As if their awareness of more *problems* in the world will actually bring them into a fuller existence. Isn't it an awe-inspiring site to watch children play? The outside world vanishes as they become completely caught up in the joy of the moment before them.

We look on at such "child's play" and think, "Those were the days..." But Jesus tells us that there's something about the innocence and fullness of life that a child has which *has to become ours* if we are to enter into everything He has for us.

He's not asking us to abandon our God-given responsibilities, but perhaps He is asking us to abandon our self-appointed ones—like the self-appointed need to make sure that no one takes advantage of us or the self-appointed role of critic—always finding the worst in people—or the self-appointed task of worrying—always seeing what *could potentially* go wrong (yet seldom ever does).

There are many characteristics children have that we tend to lack. The sad thing is that we are not focused on becoming more like them but have believed the lie that our true fulfillment will come when we are more "grown up." Growing up is, indeed, a huge part of our Christian life, but not the kind of growing up that makes us rigid, staunch, stuck in our ways, fearful, negative, or burdened. No, that's not the kind of people walking around in Heaven, for Heaven *belongs* to the *children*. May we be one of them!

God, help me to see You as a child does—believing what You say and enjoying every part of my life. Help me to not bring yesterday into today and to live with a general *unawareness* of problems, not because I am oblivious or naive, but because my faith in You *completely overshadows* any problem or person that could try to distract me from my destiny. After all, if You are *for* me, who can be *against* me (Romans 8:31)? Thank You, LORD, for being a Father who is happy when His children enjoy their lives. I am believing what Jesus said—that as I approach You with the faith of a child, revelation will open up to me that is unavailable to those who are wise in their own eyes (Matthew 11:25). I love you God. Amen.

73
Taste Before Sight

"Oh, taste and see that the LORD is good! Blessed is the man who takes refuge in Him!" **Psalm 34:8 ESV**

How *happy* is the man who takes refuge in Him. Him who? The God who is *good.* Does that mean it's possible to take refuge or place our trust in a God who is *not* good? Absolutely. Does it not seem plausible that Satan would be working overtime to try to convince us that our God is not good? So many believers today are believing a skewed view of God that He is not good. They would not *say* He is not good, but they interpret the events of the world as if there is some degree of darkness in Him.

This verse is clear—there is a purposeful order to being a happy man. If you want to be a happy man, you must take refuge in God—but not just *any* version of God you want. It must be taking refuge in God with the full belief that He is *good.* So, how do you walk in that kind of faith? It all comes down to the way you *taste* and *see.*

Notice that purposeful progression—that you must *taste* before you *see* (Psalm 34:8). How many of us are *feeding* on negative reports, bad news, false arguments, fearful thoughts, vain imaginations, and self-pity? If all we are tasting on a daily basis is what the enemy is feeding us, it's no wonder our perspective can become so skewed about God's goodness.

But this is a principle. And the way a principle works is that it is functioning even when you are not aware of it or don't believe it. So the point is, this principle remains: *Taste comes before sight.*

If taste precedes sight, then we must become keenly aware of our daily diet. Are we truly feasting upon good things? Are we focused on what God *is* doing or on what we think He's *not* doing? Are we thinking about what He *has* done or about what we think He's *failed* to do? Are we walking in delight or disappointment? Faith or fear? Victory or defeat?

Paul said it another way: "Finally, brothers, whatever is true, whatever is honorable, whatever is just, whatever is pure, whatever is lovely, whatever is commendable, if there is any excellence, if there is anything worthy of praise, think about these things" (Philippians 4:8 ESV).

Jesus said it in this fascinating verse: "Therefore consider carefully how you listen. Whoever has will be given more; whoever does not have, even what they think they have will be taken from them" (Luke 8:18).

What does He mean that *more* will be given to you according to how you listen?

Whatever you are feasting on, *more* will be brought your way! Have you ever noticed that when you listen to gossip about people, *more* juicy details continue to come your way? What about thoughts of bitterness? If you begin to listen to those, *more* keep coming. How about feasting on negativity? Oh yes, once we start looking for faults, our fault-finder beeps everywhere we turn. Why? Because it's a principle that what you are listening to or feasting on or tasting will be brought to you in *greater measure*. It's another way of saying that what you are *tasting* you will begin to *see*.

It may seem strange, but it's a spiritual principle all the same. And, it's a spiritual principle that you've surely experienced countless times, without possibly even knowing it was operating. Furthermore, it's a spiritual principle that can work to your advantage.

How so? By your own choice. Praise God that He has given us the freedom to choose and also empowered us with a gift from the Holy Spirit called "self-control" (Galatians 5:23).

So you can use this principle to your own advantage. Choose to be a person who wants to make your refuge, your hiding place, your existence in the God who is 100% good. Then, realize that to abide in Him, you must believe that He is *fully good*. And the inroad to walking in that is by choosing to *feast on* His goodness. Look for *positive* reports wherever you go. Refuse to harbor bitter thoughts. Reject negativity when it presents itself to you. Every time an argument comes to mind as to why someone or some place isn't living up to your expectations or a question comes about their motives, realize that one of the biggest weapons we have been given is the ability to cast down arguments that Satan brings to our minds. We can thankfully take every thought captive to the obedience of Christ (2 Corinthians 10:5).

Yes, God is good. He's so good that He has given us the power to choose our own thinking and what we listen to. From there, more of the same will be brought to us. Therefore, if we are feasting upon His goodness, we will begin to *see* His goodness everywhere we look. And, since we know from Scripture that "in Him there is no darkness at all" (1 John 1:5 ESV), we can be *sure* that there's an *unlimited* amount of His goodness to behold.

"We demolish arguments and every pretension that sets itself up against the knowledge of God, and we take captive every thought to make it obedient to Christ" (2 Corinthians 10:5).

God, today I praise You for Your goodness. Help me to feast upon Your goodness today and begin to see it manifest everywhere I look. Help me to break off all agreements with the enemy and no longer be someone who feasts upon negativity, bad reports, or judgment. Help me to have a steady diet of Your goodness, mercy, righteousness, peace, and joy. And, may more be brought my way. In Jesus' Name, Amen!

"For the kingdom of God is not a matter of eating and drinking but of righteousness and peace and joy in the Holy Spirit" (Romans 14:17 ESV).

74
Kings Search Out

"It is the glory of God to conceal things, but the glory of kings is to search things out." ***Proverbs 25:2 ESV***

It is the royalty in you that will refuse to live with a discontented contentment. While God desires for us to have "godliness with contentment" (1 Timothy 6:6), He is not asking us to sign up for a life of mundanity. God has a great adventure for all of us!

Sometimes we are called to seasons of quiet and rest, while at other times we hear the energizing words of God: "Go forward!" (Exodus 14:15). We must not confuse one with the other. It is the fact that you are a child of the King that makes you want to press into God's still small voice.

If the above verse about God concealing matters is taken at face value, we must come to believe that God is hiding things for us to find. He is playing His part (God) so that we will become ours (kings). Do not become discouraged or disheartened by any sense of ambiguity. God is not the author of confusion (1 Corinthians 14:33), but He is the author of adventure. And sometimes, the very breakthrough we have been waiting for—through long, quiet seasons—is just a moment away. If we would but press in and search out the things of God, we will have the confirmation of the words of Jesus in our hearts "the violent take it by force" (Matthew 11:12 ESV).

Never let go of what God has promised to you. And do not allow seasons of quietness or rest to make you question the clarity of His promise. God is able, and He will cause you to inherit what He has promised. Only allow Him to be God and by virtue of your Sonship, you will walk as a king.

75
Letting Go of Control

> *"For rebellion is as the sin of divination, and presumption is as iniquity and idolatry."* ***1 Samuel 15:23 ESV***

Divination or witchcraft is the attempt to make things happen apart from God. While some forms are extremely obvious like the worship of Satan and practicing of dark arts, others are more subtle. Yet subtlety does not lessen the reality. And if, though subtle, someone is *really* trying to control outcomes, exert control, and manufacture changes apart from God, then the consequences can be just as detrimental—or perhaps it can be even worse because when something is subtle you may not connect the dots between your practice and your results.

For example, do I try to get my children to obey by manipulation, coercion, or control? Do I try to secure my position at work or in the world through my own determined effort, worry, and carefully measured outcomes? Do I try to make sure people treat me the right way so that I don't get taken advantage of or overlooked? Do I control people through my words, looks, actions, or reactions? Do I live with a general sense that it all falls on me and that I must be ten steps ahead or I will miss heading off potential pain, failure, or loss? Too many times the answer to these questions is yes.

And when that is the case, I am not only *not* walking in simple faith and trust in the LORD, I'm also fighting a barrage of consequences for walking in unbelief.

Using control or manipulation is actually walking under the law. Sure, it's the law of your own creation, but it's a law you are following, nonetheless. The law goes something like this: If I *say* the right thing, *think* far enough into the future, *do* the right thing, or *head off* all foreseeable circumstances, then I'll be okay (have things go my way). But this has nothing to do with Christ! It is the state which the Apostle Paul described as, "You are severed from Christ, you who would be justified by the law; you have fallen away from grace" (Galatians 5:4 ESV).

The consequences of walking in control and manipulation are something that sadly, are better *felt* than *described*. Not that we would want people to experience the fallout, but often it is only once you see the fallout and how terrible life feels to try to keep everything under your thumb that you realize—*there must be a better way*! It's true, there is a better Way, but it's so radically different from how you have lived a life of control that it requires a death. A death to yourself.

"Whoever seeks to preserve his life will lose it, but whoever loses his life will keep it" (Luke 17:33 ESV).

If this is true, then what a crazy contrary reality we try to live in where we think that our main job is to *preserve* our life. No wonder so many people are discontent with their lives—they are trying to save them! But complete surrender and letting go to Christ for His sake and His way is the key to ultimate life.

Are you willing to let go to Jesus? Are you willing to start living like He is in control and that you don't have to pretend you are? Are you willing to believe that Jesus has your best interests in mind?

"The thief comes only to steal and kill and destroy. I came that they may have life and have it abundantly" (John 10:10 ESV).

Practically speaking, which reality do you feel like you are walking in? Does your life feel *abundant*? Or does it feel like things have been *stolen* and *destroyed*? That will give you great clarity as to if you have allowed manipulation and control into your life. Instead of control, we exercise faith in God by *surrender*. The tool of manipulation is always from Satan. But God has given us the tool of faith. Use it or lose it. And lose your life to find it. These realities require us to make a decisive break from our previous way of thinking, and in doing so, they will bring a tremendous amount of peace and a smooth path once we start sowing the right seeds today so we can reap tomorrow (Galatians 6:7).

76
Do Not Fear

"And free those who all their lives were held in slavery by their fear of death." **Hebrews 2:15**

Notice that the *inroad* to slavery is *fear*. If the enemy could, he would enslave us to every fear imaginable. But no greater fear has enslaved the world than the fear of death. Mortality is an awful burden unless you have been given the gift of eternal life.

What this passage tells me is that Jesus died to set me free not only from hell but from *death entirely* and not only from death but from *slavery* and not only from slavery but from *every fear* that would try to assail me.

Those who are in Christ have eternal life secured. But God also will "give life to our mortal bodies" (Romans 8:11). He gives personal words of assurance about our lives—that they will not be quickly snatched from us.

"But the LORD said to him, 'Peace be to you. Do not fear; you shall not die'" (Judges 6:23 ESV).

One time when I was fearing that I had a disease or an underlying, undetected issue that could lead to my demise, this was the verse God spoke to me. It is what He told Gideon so long ago, and yet it applied to me today. He made it personal to me.

God is so good to calm and release us from all our fears. Maybe Satan has you enslaved to fear of sudden demise, sickness, failure, disease or death. Perhaps you need a personal word today.

"With long life I will satisfy him and show him my salvation" (Psalm 91:16 ESV).

Let God's love free you from all fear (1 John 4:18) and rest in the peaceful assurance that He always has your best in mind and will never forsake you (Psalm 17:8; Hebrews 13:5).

77

What Sobers You?

"Therefore let anyone who thinks that he stands take heed lest he fall." **1 Corinthians 10:12 ESV**

There are times in life where God allows you to see someone fall or some very hard situation be made public. This should not be considered anything but God's grace to you. He desires for you to not think that you are above falling or somehow not in need of His grace.

He wants us to repent of pride and unbelief and self-dependence and self-sufficiency. When we heed these examples, He allows us to see and turn from our own pride. He brings times of refreshing to us (Acts 3:19-20). But may we never be someone who looks on at another's downfall with scoffing, judgment, or—God forbid—joy. We are never supposed to rejoice at someone's downfall.

It is a sobering thing to see another man turn away from God. It's a very sobering and sad thing—especially when it is someone who has publicly taken their stand before as a moral or pure or God-fearing individual. The only lesson such should have to us is not "see I knew there was hidden sin"—but—"God I see that I need to repent for any seeds of the same in my own life."

The above verse tells us that the only proper response for us is to "take heed" because if we don't "we too shall fall" (1 Corinthians 10:12). We should turn to the LORD and intercede for mercy for the man or woman who has found themselves in such straits. We should pray for them to be spared from shaming by the enemy, who loves to pounce on a believer's missteps and sins and expose them and magnify their faults as a way to get others to stop magnifying the LORD. You cannot both magnify another's failures and magnify the LORD at the same time (Psalm 34:3).

May we not ignore the things the LORD allows us to see, but may we grow from them. God, help us to turn to You with truly repentant hearts, expressing what Your Word says as truth—that we must take heed or else fall (1 Corinthians 10:12). We take heed of your warnings and loving probings of our hearts today, and we turn *away from* our pride, self-promotion, self-reliance, and all things *self*—turning *toward* You, our loving Father. As we do, please bring the times of tender refreshing which You have promised us. In Jesus' Name, Amen.

78
Divided Pursuit

*"For where your treasure is, there your heart will be also." **Matthew 6:21 ESV***

If we'd allow it, this is one of the most convicting verses in the New Testament. Jesus didn't say these words *flippantly* or *harshly*; however, He did say them *surgically*, purposing to get to the true devotion of our hearts.

Some questions:

What is it that you treasure?
What are you most excited about?
What do you spend your time doing or thinking about?
Where are the energies of your day invested?
Where is your true devotion?

I think we would want to say that God is number one in every area of our lives. And, perhaps at times it ebbs and flows. But the majority of us could honestly say that there are other things which have gained first place. These are identifiable by checking what things get our focus, excite us, or have our investment.

What we treasure, place our investment in, stew over or think about—Jesus said—has our *heart* also. So find out your treasure, and that's where your heart is.

And with a command to "love the LORD your God with all your heart" (Deuteronomy 6:5), it's important that we would not simply be a people who love Him with only part of it.

"Oh, magnify the LORD with me, and let us exalt His name together!" (Psalm 34:3 ESV).

Often what fills our *vision* steals our *focus*. And what steals our focus gets our *worship*. That's why the loudest voices or biggest problems often win our attention. And if we are not careful, we could become a people who are consumed by trying to put out fires instead of being consumed with the LORD.

Or even worse, we could replace God with the idols of our own creation—thinking that success, status, wealth, or even the achieving of our goals is the highest pursuit and calling we could have (as if those things could satisfy us). Why is it that we aim for things that God never called us to and shoot for stars other than the Bright Morning One (Revelation 22:16)?

"No one can serve two masters, for either he will hate the one and love the other, or he will be devoted to the one and despise the other" (Matthew 6:24 ESV).

The point is that we have a choice. It's not about how to be balanced or more measured in our approach. The choice is one or the other. We cannot have two masters. We must make sure that any area of our hearts which we have given over to another master are quickly brought back under God's rule and authority and delight. And then—we must be the kind of servants who the Master calls "friends" (John 15:15) and who He can trust unequivocally with good gifts that we will not lose our hearts to.

God, please show us the places where we have set our hearts on someone or something other than You. May our treasure be in You and not in temporal pleasures or highs which seek to distort what our calling and purpose actually is. And, as we draw close to You, teach us how to cherish and use what You give us for our own blessing as well as the blessing of others—never becoming enraptured with the gift over the Giver. In Jesus' Name, Amen.

79
He Makes Me Lie Down

"He makes me lie down in green pastures." ***Psalm 23:2 ESV***

Has it ever happened to you that God rescinded His *invitation* to lie down and instead sent a *subpoena*?

This is what David was taking about—times when God "makes us lie down" (Psalm 23:2 ESV).

These times are often unwanted in the moment but precious in the long run. In these *seasons of lying down*, He restores our soul (Psalm 23:3). They should not be shirked or shunned but embraced.

Often when we sense something is in the way of our continued progress, pursuit, plan (or just plain busyness), we like to say that it is of the devil—that the enemy is opposing us. But shouldn't we *first* go to our Father who is the One we want to give all of our *firsts* to and ask Him if this situation is from Him?

God does not give sickness, disease or calamity—no. But there are times when the way we have been driving ourselves into the ground has natural consequences. There are times when God shields us from those, but there are other times where He knows that the only way we will make a change to our lifestyle of striving is for us to experience a small reaping of what we've sown.

And other times it's not that at all, but it's circumstances that we wish would change and have not. It's not always a matter of God wanting *us* to change. Even still, in these times, He is at work in us—restoring our souls.

These are not times where we are supposed to try to figure everything out but to simply enjoy the color of the landscape. There's restoration in beholding the beauty of the LORD (Psalm 23:2-3).

May we not be a people who get discouraged by times when we are "made to lie down" but who relish in the beauty of the green pastures we once raced by.

80
Getting Appointed

"Hope deferred makes the heart sick, but a desire fulfilled is a tree of life." ***Proverbs 13:12 ESV***

Disappointments and deferred hope can make you sick both physically and spiritually—especially if they become the experiences you feed off of.

But a desire fulfilled is a *tree* of life (Proverbs 13:2 ESV).

You can keep eating from it. Long after the fulfillment has happened you can stay full from it. Our focus and consumption has to be on what victories God has won in our lives. We can either walk in perpetual sickness due to allowing disappointments to become our food or walk in perpetual health due to allowing the breakthroughs, the miracles, the victories and the faithfulness of God to be our bread.

While living a life feeding on what God has done is a vibrant way to live, the best part is that it actually attracts more of the same. Rehearsing what God has done is an invitation for God to do it again. Or, as John reports it: "For the testimony of Jesus is the spirit of prophecy" (Revelation 19:10 ESV).

In other words, rehearsing what God has done is prophetic of what He's about to do. He is the same yesterday, today, and forever (Hebrews 13:8), so His past faithfulness is both an *indicator* and an *invitation* for Him to do it again.

So what are you focused on today? Isn't it amazing that God could give us ten wonderful breakthroughs and yet if we have one thing unfulfilled, that *singular* thing becomes the focus of our day instead of the *ten*? How foolish! Let's begin to do what only makes sense—allow the ten to trump the one.

If you feed off of disappointments, you will eventually become afraid or apathetic toward stepping out again for fear of disappointment—and your faith will suffer for it. But in the Kingdom of God, *like* attracts *like*, *favor* attracts *favor*, and *breakthrough* attracts *breakthrough* (Matthew 13:12). So if you allow disappointment to fill your vision, you can be sure you'll develop a keen ability to find faults and disappointments with every person or situation that crosses your path. But the heart of a child remembers the joy of victory and believes the best—sometimes completely unaware of the faults and flaws around them. And it's an amazing thing—children are so happy! What we often consider *naive* is simply a Kingdom attitude of living with a focus on what is going *right* instead of what is going *wrong*. And more will be given besides (Matthew 13:12).

81
Intimately Knowing

"And then will I declare to them, 'I never knew you.'"
Matthew 7:23 ESV

Are we not grieved by the possibility that our *doing* for God could overtake our *knowing* Him?

Are we not stirred by the fact that there is a magnetic pull toward *accomplishment* over *intimacy*?

Have we not seen in the world thousands of mothers and fathers busying themselves outside the home and trying to make a name for themselves when their true gold was the little souls He had planted at their address?

Is there anything in our lives right now that looks like *production* without *purpose* or *religion* without *relationship*?

What percent of this madness shall we deem acceptable in our lives? 10%? 20%? How much do rote routine and self-promoting pursuits have to overtake our deep intimacy with the LORD before we declare, "Enough!"?

What will it take for us to call the fogginess that results what it actually is—*barrenness of soul*? We have to *discover* that we are disconnected before we can hope to plug back in.

When we are disconnected from the Life Source, we become dried up shrubs in the wilderness (Jeremiah 17:6). But those who trust in the LORD and draw near to Him will be like trees planted beside abundant waters (Jeremiah 17:7-8).

God, give us clarity about the nature of our true situation and wisdom to make a decisive break from the pull of self-effort, striving, and self-made living. We declare You to be our "all-in-all" and ask that You would fill every empty place in us—teaching us to walk in true intimacy with You. Forgive us for trading such an incredible gift for the cheapness that the world calls *success*. We repent and turn back to You, believing that it is truly when we lose our lives that we will find them (Matthew 10:39).

82

The Product of Our Thinking

"For God hath not given us the spirit of fear; but of power, and of love, and of a sound mind."
2 Timothy 1:7 KJV

One clear indicator of the source of our thinking is what it *produces* in us. Fear is an indicator that someone else is speaking. But the life God has for us is marked by the total absence of fear which can only be vanquished as we believe that God loves us personally (1 John 4:16-18) and that His definition of love and goodness are not twisted in any way (Psalm 34:8). We can let go and trust that God is good and that in Him there is no darkness at all (1 John 1:5).

God does not give us the spirit of fear. He gives us instead the spirit or *filling* of power, love, and a sound mind (2 Timothy 1:7).

I can think of nothing more clear to illustrate this great contrast between fear and a sound mind than the picture of the man Jesus healed in Mark 5:1-20. The man essentially was out of his mind and demon possessed to the point where no one could constrain him, not even with chains. He spent his life among the tombs screaming and cutting himself with stones—a clearly demonic practice (1 Kings 18:28).

Until one day, Jesus showed up and healed him by speaking to him. The great contrast between Satan's kingdom and God's Kingdom was shown: "When they came to Jesus, they saw the man who had been possessed by the legion of demons, sitting there, dressed and in his right mind" (Mark 5:15).

Look at the great change we see in this man who was once wrecked and ravaged by a spirit of fear. Now, by God's great love and grace, this man was given three things that he previously had no hope for obtaining:

1) *Seated* (Hebrews 10:12).

2) *Dressed* (Isaiah 61:10, Luke 15:22).

3) *In his right mind* (2 Timothy 1:7).

And now, by God's great love and grace, we can have the same. We can be seated and relaxed—resting in God, being fully clothed and covered in every way, and enjoying a sound mind. The man who sat their silently and peacefully portrayed a great image of the different kingdoms available for us to walk in. Remember, *God* has not given us a spirit of fear, but that doesn't mean that *Satan* isn't trying to. Instead, receive God's great gifts of power, love, and a sound mind.

Lean back into His arms. He's got you totally covered.

83
God's Current Word

> *"So He humbled you, allowed you to hunger, and fed you with manna which you did not know nor did your fathers know, that He might make you know that man shall not live by bread alone; but man lives by every word that proceeds from the mouth of the LORD."* **Deuteronomy 8:3 NKJV**

It has been said that "insanity is doing the same thing over and over again and expecting different results." That's true *unless it's not.* This is why it's so important to get God's *current* word about a situation. What is He *currently* saying? That's what it means to proceed from His mouth. It's not something He *used to say* but what is *current.* The word for "word" in the original language in this verse is "rhema" which means the *spoken* word of God. Are you hearing what God is *currently* saying to you?

The point is this—sometimes God tells us to do something again but expect different results. It's *not* insanity if God tells us to do it. Just think if Joshua had given up his marches around Jericho on the sixth day (Joshua 6:3-4) or if Elijah had not asked the servant to keep looking for the cloud a seventh time (1 Kings 18:43). The *result* was different, even though they *did* the same thing—because God said so.

There was a season in my life years ago where my wife and I had been placed in a hard situation in ministry, and we kept hearing God say, "Stay." Every time we would do what He had said and yet kept getting the same results. For three and a half years, He kept saying, "Stay." And then one day, the season changed, and His word to us was, "Go." The lessons learned in those three and a half years were integral to the destiny He had planned for us, but we would not have learned them if we had simply focused on results. Also, we would not have entered the new season if we had not stayed sensitive to His voice. The real question is, what is God *currently* saying?

God may have a *new* word for you today the way He did for David who had the wherewithal (and listening ear (Psalm 40:6)) to not rush into battle with the *previous* word God said—but sought God's *current* word and was victorious (2 Samuel 5:19-25).

Don't simply focus on the results. Don't live by logic alone. Is God telling you to march around one more time? Is He saying to go look for the cloud a seventh time? If you rely on past experiences alone you will be misled. The real question is and will always be: *What is God currently saying?*

"Remember not the former things, nor consider the things of old. Behold, I am doing a new thing; now it springs forth, do you not perceive it? I will make a way in the wilderness and rivers in the desert" (Isaiah 43:18-19 ESV).

God, please help us discern and receive every word that proceeds from Your mouth. Help us not give up, even though it may feel like insanity when you tell us to go up again, endure, or stay when the results have previously yielded nothing. Your will be done in our lives, in Jesus' Name. Amen!

84
Quiet Assurance

"Suddenly a furious storm came up on the lake, so that the waves swept over the boat. But Jesus was sleeping." ***Matthew 8:24***

It absolutely amazes me to see what Jesus did in the storm. But possibly even more amazing is what Jesus *didn't do* in the storm. He didn't panic. He didn't start ordering people around. He didn't even try to come up with a plan. He simply moved from the authority and position He already had.

And the sheer reality of this convicting story is that if Jesus sleeps in the storm then so can you.

Jesus personified something that we know we *could have* in Him—that quiet hush of assurance that all will work out according to plan. And though we may confess this as our belief, often when the storms come, we forget it entirely. Jesus shows us just how practical—though seemingly impractical—this quiet trust in God should be. Jesus chooses to not respond to the storm the way most people would. Many people would look on at a sleeper in a boat and call it "not living in reality" at best or "irresponsible" at worst. But nothing could be further from the truth. Jesus was not modeling irresponsible living, and He was more rooted in reality than anyone could know. It's just that His reality was a heavenly one which entirely overshadowed any earthly reality that seemed to threaten in that moment.

"He replied, 'You of little faith, why are you so afraid?' Then He got up and rebuked the winds and the waves, and it was completely calm" (Matthew 8:26).

A rebuke to the winds but a rebuke to us! Was Jesus expecting these disciples to sleep too? Perhaps if they had all slept, the storm would have passed with never a sound or disturbance.

It wasn't that Jesus was unaware or didn't care of their sorrows and trouble in this storm—quite the opposite. It was that, in the middle of the storm, He was giving them a gift—*access* to true rest and trust—that they otherwise could never have had. And, though obtained in a trial, they could keep and carry this present with them wherever they went for the rest of their lives—including countless victories and ultimate glory.

"Therefore, since the promise of entering His rest still stands, let us be careful that none of you be found to have fallen short of it" (Hebrews 4:1).

85
New Seasons

"Forget the former things; do not dwell on the past. See, I am doing a new thing! Now it springs up; do you not perceive it? I am making a way in the wilderness and streams in the wasteland." ***Isaiah 43:18-19***

It is often incredibly difficult to let the past seasons go and move into a new one. Sometimes we fear that if we let go, we will regret or miss what we leave behind. Many people, upon turning 30 or 40 or 50 or 60, squirm at the thought of leaving their previous decade behind. But the truth of the matter is that there are things in your 50's that you could not obtain in your 40's. And if you stay there (mentally attached to the past), you risk missing the *current* work God wants to do in this new season.

Leaving behind the old may be hard, but it is necessary if we are to enter into all that God has for us.

The above verse *commands* us to stop dwelling on the past and start looking at what God is *currently* doing. If we are so set on staying where we are and continuing in the current situation, we risk not *perceiving* the beautiful things God is doing right now. "Do you not perceive it?" (Isaiah 43:19). Well, you may not if you don't let go of what is dead and surrender to the new season God has for you.

When I got married I had a revelation that I was no longer able to live a bachelor life and stay out late with my friends or play sports at dinnertime or any manner of other things that no longer fit with the current schedule of being a husband. For the longest time I had false guilt because I was unable to give to my friends the same amount of attention and time that I previously had—until I realized this truth.

We never need to be ashamed of the season that God has us in. We will live with the most energy and enthusiasm when we fully embrace the calling, purpose, and role that God has for us *today.*

"For everything there is a season, and a time for every matter under heaven" (Ecclesiastes 3:1 ESV).

A season and a time...for *everything.*

Solomon, the wisest man who ever lived said this. And since that's the case, it bears recognizing that one of the most important things we could ever do is discern what *season* God has us in. What purpose does He have for us going forward—not looking back?

Every so often, God will prompt us to ask that question. It's wise even, to slow down, quiet ourselves, and ask God if we are trying to walk in a season or timing that is outside of His. Perhaps it's something that He at one time clearly led us to, and we thought that one word was *forever* instead of *seasonal.*

Either way, we know for sure that humans have been labeled "creatures of habit." For that very reason, we risk getting *stuck in the same* and missing the new all because we like the comfort of "normal" and the control that comes with "sameness."

So what about you? What season does God have you in? Is He asking you to let go of something from a previous season, a previous disappointment, a previous person? God's best for us does not lie in the past, but ahead (Jeremiah 29:11). And if we keep our minds in the past, it is only because we don't believe that God has a better future ahead of us.

We don't want to assume that we should keep doing the same things simply because we felt led to it before.

Even David after just winning in battle, refused to go up against the enemy in the same way or assume a victory just because it had happened already. Instead, he sought the LORD and God gave him a different battle plan for victory. If he had rushed ahead assuming that the same strategy would work, it could have been devastating (2 Samuel 5:19-25).

May God give us clarity about the season, strategy, and purpose He has for us—not yesterday but *today*.

86
God's View of You

"For I am honored in the eyes of the LORD, and my God has become my strength." ***Isaiah 49:5 ESV***

Honored.

Is this the way that you view *God's* view of you?

Have you become convinced of this—that you are *honored* in the eyes of the LORD? Has the mass of voices shouting to the contrary convinced you otherwise?

Even deeper, has God become your *strength*? This cannot happen until the revelation of His love has occurred. That's why it's the *joy of the LORD* that is our strength (Nehemiah 8:10). Do you realize that you are His joy and crown (Philippians 4:1) and that He rejoices over you with singing (Zephaniah 3:17)?

Is your view of yourself representative of His view of you? Surprisingly, this will largely determine how other people view you.

"And there we saw the Nephilim (the sons of Anak, who come from the Nephilim), and we seemed to ourselves like grasshoppers, and so we seemed to them" (Numbers 13:33 ESV).

Today, even when there are voices whispering otherwise, be convinced of this one thing: You are *honored* in the eyes of the LORD.

87
Feeding on Faithfulness

"Then Samuel took a stone and set it up between Mizpah and Shen. He named it Ebenezer, saying, 'Thus far the LORD has helped us.'" **1 Samuel 7:12**

Do we not often look ahead into the future with worry instead of focusing on God's faithfulness along the way?

"Trust in the LORD, and do good; dwell in the land and feed on faithfulness" (Psalm 37:3 ESV).

Are you feeding on the faithfulness of God, or are you troubled about the future? Can you look at the circumstance or issue which is rearing its ugly head in your life and with confidence say, "Thus far the LORD has helped me" (1 Samuel 7:12)?

We must embrace both the past lessons and movements of God to operate fully in the divine calling before us *now*. We teach our children that they don't need to be afraid of the dark, but that's because we have experienced it time and time again. Should we not have that same confidence when the lights seem to go out in our own lives?

Far be it from us to forget the great works of the LORD in our lives!

"Bless the LORD, O my soul, and forget not all His benefits" (Psalm 103:2 ESV).

It is a healthy practice to, from time to time, pause and direct our thoughts simply toward all that God has done in our lives. It is always a healing experience to focus on His wonderful faithfulness and kindness toward us. And, once we position ourselves in the faithfulness and goodness of God, we will be able to go forward with great faith into the future knowing that God will never leave us or forsake us (Hebrews 13:5).

May we not forget even *one* of His benefits!

88
Stay in the Party

"The older brother became angry and refused to go in. So his father went out and pleaded with him." ***Luke 15:28***

What to do with jealousy?

When someone is jealous of you, your position or your life situation, the thing you must never do is leave the party. The enemy tries to sow seeds of jealousy into people's minds—not simply to destroy *their* life with jealousy but to ruin *your* party as well. Jealousy consumes from the inside out—but without a doubt—it will work it's way out.

The crazy thing about Luke 15 is that the son who was jealous was upset about never getting a *goat*, but his father ends up telling him that he owns the whole *farm* (Luke 15:31).

Healing from jealousy starts with realizing that we are not part of an orphanage but a family. There is more than enough to go around. All can have their fill—for Christ Himself fills all in all (Ephesians 1:23).

So if you struggle with jealousy it's not because someone has more than you but because you do not realize what you are in possession of.

God has given us *everything* we need for life and godliness. (2 Peter 1:3).

He has blessed us with *every* spiritual blessing (Ephesians 1:3).

He delights in giving good gifts to His children (Matthew 7:11).

And if you are being ridiculed by a jealous spirit, no worries.

Never embrace false guilt for experiencing the favor of the LORD.

It is not your job to plead with a jealous person. That would only be succumbing to manipulation. Rather, let the Father go out and plead with them to come into the very party He has thrown in your honor (Luke 15:28). And, when the time comes for *their* party, be sure that you have learned the pivotal command to rejoice with those who rejoice (Romans 12:15).

89
Worth the Wait

"And David spoke to the LORD the words of this song on the day when the LORD delivered him from the hand of all his enemies, and from the hand of Saul."
2 Samuel 22:1 ESV

God never forgets the pain we have been through.

Even when healing comes, God remembers all that we have endured on the way to our destiny. And in a way, it was this very path which has prepared us to steward what will be given to us.

It has been said that Saul was given the Kingdom in a day and lost it. David took years (over a decade) through the wilderness, living in a cave, and dodging the spears of those who throw them—only because they have not learned how to rejoice with those who rejoice (Romans 12:15) or father someone who has favor on their life (1 Corinthians 4:15).

David had to endure the false accusations of those closest to him—without the ability to change their mind. He wandered down a road that many of us would not envy.

And yet, he wandered down a road that, although hard, was *the path to the palace.*

And so it is for those whose destiny is bigger than their imagination.

The preparation of all things higher than us should be left to God for "such knowledge is too wonderful" (Psalm 139:6).

We must not demand an answer as to why there are those who will reject us despite our motives to bless. We must simply leave the path to God. Their disdain and the trials that have ensued cannot deter us from our destiny.

"The mind of man plans his way, but the LORD directs his steps" (Proverbs 16:9 NASB).

Often, that direction seems unplanned or random—but that couldn't be further from the truth. God has carefully measured and planned all that we will need for life and godliness (2 Peter 1:3) to walk in the destiny prepared for us before we were born (Psalm 139:16, Ephesians 2:10).

May we not try to undo His ways but receive the character and depth of trust as someone who has an inheritance beyond our wildest imaginations. After all, there was a time —a singular day—when David received *total deliverance* from *all* of his enemies (2 Samuel 22:1). And I have no doubt that his deep sentiment was that it was totally *worth the wait*. How else could he declare:

"You have delivered me from the attacks of the peoples; You have preserved me as the head of nations. People I did not know now serve me, foreigners cower before me; as soon as they hear of me, they obey me. They all lose heart; they come trembling from their strongholds. The LORD lives! Praise be to my Rock! Exalted be my God, the Rock, my Savior! He is the God who avenges me, who puts the nations under me, who sets me free from my enemies. You exalted me above my foes; from a violent man You rescued me. Therefore I will praise You, LORD, among the nations; I will sing the praises of Your name. He gives His king great victories; He shows unfailing kindness to His anointed, to David and his descendants forever" (2 Samuel 22:44-51).

90

My Feelings Are Not My Master

> *"Just before dawn Paul urged them all to eat. 'For the last fourteen days,' he said, 'you have been in constant suspense and have gone without food—you haven't eaten anything. Now I urge you to take some food. You need it to survive. Not one of you will lose a single hair from his head.' After he said this, he took some bread and gave thanks to God in front of them all. Then he broke it and began to eat. They were all encouraged and ate some food themselves."* **Acts 27:33-36**

One of the most critical lessons we could learn as believers in Jesus is that my feelings are not my master. There is a higher reality that defines me than my feelings. Often, I diagnose how I'm doing by how I feel, and that is exactly how the enemy would have it.

For a shift to occur in the feelings department, something has to change in the thinking department (Romans 12:2). The most important change in our thinking has to do with our view of God, His character, His nature, and His love for us.

Ultimately, if we view any situation with a flawed view of God, we open ourselves up to the lies of the enemy. This is why Paul instructs us to *fix our eyes on Jesus* (Hebrews 12:2) and why Jesus tells us that the things we are *after* come *after* we are solely *after* Him (Matthew 6:33).

Knowing God—His nature, His character, and His intimacy—is vital in receiving the peace that *surpasses* understanding

(Philippians 4:7) in the same way that *you don't have to understand how the ship works if you know the Captain.*

Speaking of ships, the above story is fascinating. All the men on the ship believed they were headed for their death except for Paul. Out of his *intimacy* with the Lord, Jesus told him that everything would be okay. And here's the really amazing thing—*Paul believed* God *even when it didn't look like it was true.*

"So keep up your courage, men, for I have faith in God that it will happen just as He told me" (Acts 27:25).

And from this encouragement, he encouraged others.

91
His Favor Rests

"For His anger lasts only a moment, but His favor lasts a lifetime..." ***Psalm 30:5***

It is interesting how we can get so focused on God's *anger* which is only for a *moment* instead of His *favor* which lasts a *lifetime.*

Do we live with a greater sense of His anger or favor? Do we walk with the confidence that we have His favor for our whole lives?

"May the favor of the Lord our God rest on us; establish the work of our hands for us—yes, establish the work of our hands" (Psalm 90:17).

Indeed it does *rest*. God's favor has come to *stay*. In fact, in Scripture when something is doubled it often means it's certain (Genesis 41:32). I don't need to try to work up anything or impress anyone, God's favor will *rest* upon me and establish the work of my hands. Yes, establish the work of my hands.

God, let that prayer be our prayer and focus today: "May the favor of the Lord our God rest on us; establish the work of our hands for us—yes, establish the work of our hands" (Psalm 90:17).

92
Saved by His Life

> *"For if, while we were God's enemies, we were reconciled to Him through the death of His Son, how much more, having been reconciled, shall we be saved through His life!"* ***Romans 5:10***

Jesus is everything that I am not, and in a strange way, everything that I am—my core identity.

So much of the enemy's efforts to get us off track center on shifting our focus onto ourselves. This is why the writer of Hebrews gives us the command to fix our eyes on Jesus (Hebrews 12:2). He both authors and perfects our story.

"...fixing our eyes on Jesus, the author and perfecter of faith" (Hebrews 12:2 NASB).

We know that when we are weak, through Jesus we are actually strong (2 Corinthians 12:11).

Have we paused to consider that our fullness of life rests in Him being *everything* to us that we are not?

Instead of my lack of faith, my hope is in *His* complete faithfulness. Instead of my abundance of fear, my focus is *His* abundance of peace.

To live is Christ (Philippians 1:21), and that's why it's imperative that we learn the simplicity of abiding in Him (John 15:4). But so much of abiding in Jesus is simply *beholding* Him. We only become like Jesus as we behold Him for who He is (1 John 3:2). But without beholding Him, all we are left to do is to perform and strive and suffer and fail, thinking that He is *the standard to live up to* rather than *the life to live through us*.

What an amazing thought—if we were saved so much by His *death*, how much more shall we be saved by His *life* (Romans 5:10)?!

Thank you, God, that the focus is not on my ability to perform but on the life of Jesus who has all the faith that I could ever need. May I learn to behold the Prince of Peace and in so doing, become a brother in likeness. Thank You, Jesus, for being everything that I'm not, and in the tension of that revelation, everything that I am. Amen!

93
Working vs. Trusting

"However, to the one who does not work but trusts God who justifies the ungodly, their faith is credited as righteousness." ***Romans 4:5***

It seems that we have yet to fully embrace this. Our error is in thinking that God still needs our help to bring His promises to pass. We are grateful when He chooses to use us and work through us, but it never comes from self-initiative or self-dependence.

Martha had to learn the lesson that her sister Mary had already embraced (Luke 10:42)—the real miracle comes only when we choose to "not work but trust" (Romans 4:5).

Has it not been made clear to us in times past, when coming to the "end of our rope" so to speak, we leaned our entire hopes on God moving on our behalf? Why do we often wait until we *cannot* work to figure out that *faith comes not by doing but by hearing* (Romans 10:17)? But we often cannot *hear* when the *noise* of our human effort shouts over the still small voice of God (1 Kings 19:12).

Instead, while we have the *ability* to work, why not rather choose to exercise full belief in God's ability, timing, and ways by taking a Sabbatical from our efforts, wholly entrusting ourselves to Him? We will indeed find that God is true to His Word and is waiting to be gracious to us (Isaiah 30:18).

The heart and life of a believer is to show that we do not place our hope in ourselves but in God whose faithfulness is not tied to our performance but on His character and His love for us.

94
He Starts and Finishes

> *"Fixing our eyes on Jesus, the author and perfecter of faith."* ***Hebrews 12:2 NASB***

Author.

Perfecter.

These are two new attributes to consider other than *Savior*. Praise God that He *saves*! But also praise God that Jesus *finishes* what He *starts* and is the true Beginning and Author of all things good in our lives (James 1:17).

He *starts* and *finishes.*

The real question of our day is: What are we trying to *author* or *perfect* apart from Him?

95
The LORD Will Fulfill His Purpose

"The LORD will fulfill His purpose for me." ***Psalm 138:8 ESV***

When feeling low and not sure of your calling or path, remember: *The LORD will fulfill His purpose for you* (Psalm 138:8 ESV).

If there seems to be little that excites you or moves you today, lean on this—God has *promised* to fulfill His purposes for you.

You don't need to fear missing out. You don't need to fear a less-than-stellar existence. God has preplanned for you and ordered your life in such a way that your purpose—knit into your heart from before you were born—*will be carried out* (Psalm 139:13).

This one simple truth should be celebrated and bring refreshment to your soul—knowing that it's *God's job* to bring you into the fullness of your destiny and that will always mean walking totally in His purpose for your life. Leave it with Him and rejoice that it's in totally capable hands!

96
The Danger of Overthinking

> *"Such knowledge is too wonderful for me; it is high; I cannot attain it."* ***Psalm 139:6 ESV***

Sometimes we are in danger of overthinking. We feel that we must understand *everything* to have peace. But the Bible promises that there is a peace that *surpasses* understanding (Philippians 4:7).

This doesn't mean that we understand *nothing* or that having understanding about something is wrong. It just means that we are not to *lean on* our understanding (Proverbs 3:5).

Instead, we must trust in the LORD with all of our hearts and acknowledge Him in all of our ways (Proverbs 3:5-6).

As hard as it may be at times when limitless thoughts flood our minds—about the future, about the past, or perhaps about things that we cannot quite figure out—sometimes the very *best* thing we can do is to focus more on the state of our hearts than our heads.

Is my heart *trusting* in the LORD? Is it *soft* toward Him? *Leaning* upon Him? *Surrendered* to Him? *Trusting* in Him? And then, putting a *voice* to our hearts, we simply acknowledge God: *God, I trust You and I acknowledge You, even if I do not have understanding in the current moment. I honor You, God, and I ask You to direct my steps as I continue to lean upon You. Amen!*

97
Simplicity & Sincerity

> *"For our boast is this, the testimony of our conscience, that we behaved in the world with simplicity and godly sincerity, not by earthly wisdom but by the grace of God, and supremely so toward you."* **2 Corinthians 1:12 ESV**

Simplicity and *sincerity.*

Can we say that our conscience also tells us we are living a *simple* and *sincere* life? Or are we living by earthly wisdom?

Living by grace is the opposite of living by earthly wisdom—living by grace toward others and *ourselves.*

This goes against the world system which says a wise person must be constantly achieving, doing, earning, learning, and striving. But the grace of God calls us to live lives as *sincere* people— not pretending or putting on a show and living with *simplicity*—not making things so complicated.

When was the last time you weren't rushed? Looked at the sunset? Sat on your porch? Took a long nap? Walked down a trail? Listened to music you enjoy? Just sat *still*?

We often feel like time not spent *accomplishing* is time wasted. But that's worldly wisdom and at best it can make your soul *empty* and your schedule *full.* God's grace, on the other hand, gives us room to *breathe* and *rest.* And from that place of rest and trust, God will do *amazing* things in our lives.

Don't go out and try to accomplish *for* God. Rest *in Him*—He is the Master Builder, the Author and Perfecter, the Beginning and End (1 Corinthians 3:10-11, Hebrews 12:2, Revelation 22:13).

Stay with Him!

Appendix: Who Are You?

> *"He came and preached* ***peace to you who were far away*** *and* ***peace to those who were near****."* **Ephesians 2:17**

The great news is that Jesus doesn't wait for us to clean up our act before He offers us His peace. In fact, we cannot clean up anything in our lives without Him doing it (1 Thessalonians 5:14). Jesus is preaching peace to you today whether or not you consider yourself close to Him. He wants you to know that no matter how far away you are, His peace is still possible for you if you would *come*.

> *"****Come to me****, all you who are weary and burdened,* ***and I will give you rest****."* **Matthew 11:28**

One of my hopes for writing this devotional was that God would show you *who* He has made you to be and give you clarity about *what* He is calling you to do.

But ultimately, the Bible teaches us that our life is found in Christ (Colossians 3:4) and that we are to fix our eyes and sights upon Him alone (Hebrews 12:2).

In other words, if you're *with Him*, you'll know *who* you are —you become a child of God. *He* becomes your identity, and you will never again need the approval of another person for fulfillment.

The crisis of our day is a culture filled with people who do not know who they really are. I know from experience that not being grounded as a son or daughter of God produces a roller-coaster existence:

> *"That we may no longer be children, **tossed to and fro by the waves**."* **Ephesians 4:14 ESV**

Does your life ever feel this way—*tossed to and fro by the waves?* I have good news for you. It doesn't have to!

God has created the provision we need to become His sons and daughters by sending His Son Jesus to die on the cross for us.

Now please hear me out. I have met *many* people who never realized that the Bible says we must *accept* Jesus to be saved from our sins and become God's children:

> *"Yet to all who did **receive Him**, to those who **believed in His name**, He gave the right to become children of God."* **John 1:12**

To become children of God, we simply need to *receive* Jesus. The above verse shows us that "receiving Jesus" actually means "believing in His name" (John 1:12). Simply put, this means accepting Him entirely, including all that He has done for us.

I have interacted with hundreds of college students and adults alike who thought that going to church meant they had a relationship with God. They were under the impression that church attendance would get them into heaven when they died.

But the Bible is clear:

> *"If you **declare with your mouth,** 'Jesus is Lord,' **and believe in your heart** that God raised Him from the dead, you will be saved."* **Romans 10:9**

Have you made this decision? Have you made this confession and believed in your heart that Jesus died, was buried, and was raised for *you?*

He did all of this to pay for your sins and bring you into a son or daughter relationship with God!

> *"Suppose one of you has a hundred sheep and loses one of them.* ***Doesn't he leave the ninety-nine*** *in the open country* ***and go after the lost sheep*** *until he finds it?"* **Luke 15:4**

It may be easy to believe that God loves the *world* or died for *other people's* sins, but the Bible teaches that He did it for *you.* He left the ninety-nine to come after the one. And guess what? *You are the one!* The focus isn't on what He has done for everyone else but for *you.*

If you have never invited Jesus into your heart by repenting of your sins and believing that He paid for them on the cross, would you pray this prayer right now?

> *Dear God,*
>
> *I confess to You that I have not lived the way You desire. I have sinned against You, and for that, I am truly sorry. I am making a decision today to once and for all place my faith in what Jesus has done for me. I want to be Your son/daughter. Please forgive me for all of my sins. I confess that Jesus died, was buried, and rose from the dead for me. I invite You today to be my Savior, my Lord, my Father, and my Friend.*
>
> *In Jesus' Name,*
> *Amen*

If you sincerely prayed that prayer, I believe that God—who cannot lie (Titus 1:2)—has been faithful to His Word, and you have become His child! Congratulations! This is the best and most life-changing decision you could ever make.

My suggestion to you is to get into a good, Bible-teaching church and grow in your relationship with the LORD. May you become a person who is so grounded in your identity with God that you are "no longer tossed to and fro by the waves" (Ephesians 4:14 ESV).

God bless you!
Wes Raley

About The Author:

Wes and his wife Korie live in Indiana with their children. They believe that God still speaks today and that "He is not far from any one of us" (Acts 17:27). Together they lead a ministry platform called Words That Proceed (**wordsthatproceed.com**) where they help people to hear from God, believe what He is saying, and walk in His plan for their lives.

***If you enjoyed this book, would you please consider taking a moment to review it on Amazon? That would help us so much! Thank you!**

He Sat Down (So You Can Too)

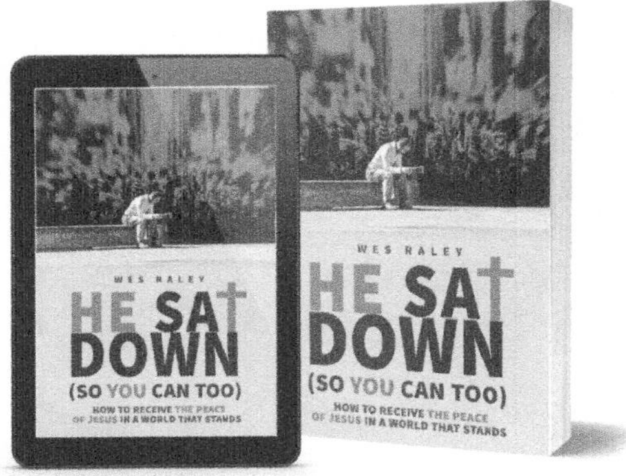

Amazon #1 Best Seller

Be done with a life of striving, stress, and anxious toil.

Available now on Amazon

Made in the USA
Coppell, TX
28 January 2021

48955326R00125